William Randolph
HEARST

An Illustrated Biography

by
Nancy E. Loe

ALBION
PUBLISHING GROUP

© 1988, 1993, 1998 by
Aramark Leisure Services, Inc.
All rights reserved. Published 1988
Second Printing 1993
Third Printing 1998

Hearst Castle
P.O. Box 210
San Simeon, CA 93452-0210
(805) 927-8601
aramark@callamerica.net

Produced by
Albion Publishing Group
Santa Barbara, CA
(805) 963-6004

Research Consultant: Denise K. Fourie
Design by Don French & Associates, Santa Barbara

Edited by Carey Vendrame

Typesetting by Tom Buhl Typographers, Santa Barbara

Printed in Singapore through Asiaprint Ltd. USA

Library of Congress Catalog Card Number: 87-70961
ISBN 1-880352-35-4

ILLUSTRATION CREDITS

ACKNOWLEDGEMENTS

The opportunity to acknowledge the assistance of one's friends and colleagues in a book must be equivalent to an actor's windy acceptance speech at the Academy Awards. The temptation is strong to thank everyone from my accountant to my yoga instructor, but instead my deepest gratitude goes to four important people: Denise Fourie, Robert Pavlik, Mary Weaver, and Kathleen Young.

Denise Fourie, who researched photos and text for this book, provided me with a varied and inexhaustible supply of resources as well as her tremendous organizational sense. Her abilities as a reference librarian are unequalled by any other professional I know. Her pithy and direct comments on the drafts of this book were gratefully received, but she may refuse to work with me in the future unless I disable the hyphen key on my personal computer.

Bob Pavlik read each successive draft of the book with patience and infinite care. I believe it is a tribute to his thoughtful comments, diplomatic personality, and sense of humor that we began this project as colleagues and ended up as friends. His perspective as a professional historian immeasurably improved the text and his foreword provides a succinct summation of the ideas I attempt to link to Hearst's life.

Mary Weaver and Kathleen Young, my co-workers in the Special Collections and University Archives Department of the Robert E. Kennedy Library at Cal Poly, literally gave me the help I needed to complete this project. Many of my regular responsibilities were taken on willingly by these two women, providing me with the time and energy to make this book a reality. Mary dispensed her unique blend of common sense and sympathy at precisely the right moments. Kathie deciphered more illegible handwriting belonging to Hearst family members than either she or I care to remember.

Among my colleagues, Dr. Bonnie Hardwick, Peter Hanff and Richard Ogar, all of The Bancroft Library, provided me with unstinting assistance during a very busy period. Linda Mehr, Sam Gill, and Stacy Endres of the Academy of Motion Picture Arts and Sciences also extended me every professional courtesy. Sandra Buchman and Carolyn Martin gave me access to the archival material held at the Hearst San Simeon State Historical Monument.

Robert Board was extremely generous with both his time and his mammoth collection of vintage material on Marion Davies. Without his help I could not have even attempted to explore Hearst's Hollywood connections. John Coghlan was gracious to allow access to and reproduction of the "funny sides" drawn by his great-grandfather, R.F. Outcault.

In addition, I am grateful to my good friend and master wordsmith, Martha Arends, who saved me from some truly egregious grammatical and syntactical errors while condensing and clarifying my unwieldy prose. Guy Rathbun sorted out some mysteries about popular music in the 1920s and played all my favorites on his KCBX radio program when I worked late on Friday nights.

Others who provided unhesitating assistance and support are: Kathleen Atkinson, Rosemary Donnell, Jon Duim, Lynne Gamble, Madeline George, Jean Gordon, Mark Schecter, Janice Stone, Teana Suggs-Chandler, and Brian Williams.

Nancy Loe
San Luis Obispo, California
April 29, 1987

For A. K. A.

"We shall not cease from exploration
And the end of all our exploring
Will be to arrive where we started
And to know the place for the first time."

—T. S. Eliot

CONTENTS

FIFTEEN CENTS

August 15, 1927

TIME

The Weekly Newsmagazine

WILLIAM RANDOLPH HEARST

"Let us not be too hard on fools."

(See THE PRESS)

Volume X

Number 7

FOREWORD

In his 1961 biography of William Randolph Hearst entitled *Citizen Hearst,* W.A. Swanberg called his subject "The Great American Enigma." Twenty-six years later, examining the 88 year lifespan of a man who was applauded and defamed, praised and cursed, Swanberg's characterization remains an accurate assessment.

Hearst was born during the height of the Civil War in the Barbary Coast town of San Francisco to parents of recent and substantial wealth. At the age of 10, he and his mother traveled the length of the continent on the recently completed transcontinental railroad. Continuing on to Europe, they visited the cultural and historical sites of the Old World in the first wave of Americans who were making the Grand Tour. By the time he was a teenager, young Will was living on both coasts, an unusual distinction for any American, even a century later. As a young man he epitomized the era that came to be regarded as America's Gilded Age.

At the same time, Will's father, George Hearst, was busily exploring and acquiring both mineral and land wealth across the American West, boosting the family's fortune to astronomical sums. Will's mother and the family's matriarch, Phoebe Apperson Hearst, directed the cultural refinement and education of her only child, while playing the role of hostess and benefactress to countless individuals and organizations. At the age of 23, William Randolph Hearst was granted ownership of his father's newspaper, the San Francisco *Examiner,* on March 4, 1887. This seemingly simple exchange between father and son

would, in years to come, develop into one of the most powerful and influential media dynasties that this country has ever known.

William Randolph Hearst's modest yet disappointing foray into politics, his enthusiastic embrace of motion picture technology, and his enormous appetite for antiquities, combined with an equally intense passion for directing simultaneous building projects, marks this man of liberal taste and infinite interests as one of the most energetic, far-reaching, and complex individuals of our time. To capture, convey, and evaluate the essence of such an individual is no easy task.

Nancy Loe has done just that. An accomplished archivist and librarian at California Polytechnic State University, San Luis Obispo, Loe has reassessed the life of William Randolph Hearst in terms of his boyhood and youth, as well as his work in his various industries, including newspapers, motion pictures, and newsreels. She also emphasizes his role as a Californian, and his ties to the state's physical, social, and cultural developments. Loe gives fresh insights into an individual far too complex and powerful in 20th century America to be remembered only for his extravagant creation at San Simeon, or his personal relationships. In his time, he influenced a nation and helped to shape its destiny , not as a politician, but as a journalist, newsmaker, observer, and activist.

During his life, Hearst forwarded the causes of many movements, individuals, and organizations. One cause that the Hearst family pioneered, both

materially and spiritually, was the cultural and social development of California. Phoebe and William Randolph Hearst's generous support and contributions to the University of California is one example of their dedication to education.

Their involvement with the reconstruction of the city of San Francisco after its terrible earthquake and fire, that city's international celebration of the opening of the Panama Canal nine years later, and the Hearst family's very personal gift to the people of the state of California, La Cuesta Encantada, all serve as reminders of our debt to this family of far-sighted philanthropists. In addition, their support of numerous artists and writers, and later, movie actors and producers, has left an indelible mark on the region as a sign of its cultural coming of age.

It is appropriate that America produced this Gilded Age Renaissance Man on its western shore. It is important that we renew and reevaluate our understanding of this dynamic Californian, who came to represent not only the energy of his age but also the prevalent vision of California as inheritor of the world's great artistic, literary, and architectural accomplishments. Loe's book is an important contribution to our on-going effort to more accurately and insightfully interpret the life, times, and accomplishments of William Randolph Hearst.

Robert C. Pavlik
Historian
San Simeon Region
Department of Parks and Recreation

Part 1

THE EARLY YEARS

William Randolph Hearst has been the subject of eight full-length biographies, as well as countless interviews, articles and reminiscences. His impact in the fields of journalism and politics has been analyzed (to different conclusions) in numerous scholarly theses and dissertations. Both novelists and screenwriters have found Hearst's diversity of interests to be rich material for several thinly disguised accounts of his life and career. Even the average citizen is drawn into his past, for almost a million tourists travel each year to the Central California coast to visit his "castle."

The founder of the Hearst family in America was John Hurst, a Scottish Presbyterian who arrived in Virginia in 1680, and settled in Isle of Wight County. The Old English spelling of the name was "Hyrst," meaning a group of trees or a thicket. After two generations in America, the family is found in Bertie County, North Carolina, where the English spelling of Hurst is changed to Hearst. John Hurst's grandson, John Hearst III, married Elizabeth Knox and moved to Abbeville County, South Carolina in 1776.

John and Elizabeth Knox Hearst's third son, George, left South Carolina in 1808 for a homestead in the recently acquired Louisiana Purchase. Land along the Meramec River, not far from present day Sullivan, Missouri, attracted the first George Hearst, as it suited the twin family interests: livestock production and mining. He brought his wife and two sons, William G. and Joseph, westward to the frontier property where they prospered.

William G. Hearst married Elizabeth Collins in 1817. On September 3, 1820, their first child, George Hearst, was born on the family's original Missouri farm and named for his South Carolina pioneer grandfather. At the time George Hearst was born, his family was the most prosperous in Meramec Township, owning at least 120 acres of land and 19 slaves. Although George was raised and worked primarily on the farm, his interest in mining was sparked by the prospectors his father hired to work claims on the family land. After limited local schooling, George Hearst studied mining at the Franklin County Mining School in 1838. He is remembered by neighbors as "a raw country youth of 19 [who] tramped the hills and hollows barefooted, pantaloons rolled up to the knees, amusing himself by chasing hogs from their midday baths, cool[ing] his

Left: Phoebe Apperson Hearst with her first and only child, William Randolph Hearst.

Above: Phoebe Hearst presented this baby book designed by Charles Frederick Eaton to friends with newborns.

blistered feet in the muddy depths of the hog wallow."[1]

In November of 1844, William G. Hearst died, leaving a widow, Elizabeth; a daughter, Martha; and two sons, George and Jacob. Hearst's will described Jacob as "rendered helpless by disease" and made provisions for his care and support. In less than two years Jacob also was dead. In 1848 Elizabeth Collins Hearst remarried, taking as her husband a postmaster and former county judge, Joseph Funk.

A year later, news of the California gold strikes reached Missouri, and George was no longer content managing the family land and other business holdings. He said his farewells to his family and headed west. Six women and eight other men, including his cousins, Joseph and James Clark, comprised the overland group.

Many hazards threatened westward travelers, but dread of Indians and fear of sickness were uppermost in the minds of those on the California trail. Although Hearst avoided difficulty with Indians, he did contract a severe case of cholera. Chills, insatiable thirst, stomach pains, cramped legs and diarrhea halted his horseback progress after about a month on the trail. He became separated from his cousins and the rest of the original

Missouri party, who were forced to continue without him. Hearst recovered sufficiently to be able to mount his horse and ride, although he was still quite ill. After several days of hard travel, he rejoined the Missourians.

The Fourth of July, an important holiday for emigrants who had left the United States behind when they headed west, found George Hearst and his fellow travelers in Fort Laramie. Not daring to sacrifice a whole day to the holiday celebration, they had an extended noonday meal, topped off with St. Louis brandy, the firing of guns and a spirited rendition of the National Anthem.

They resumed their journey, spurred by talk of bad weather, stories of the Donner Party tragedy four winters earlier, and conflicting reports that the gold country was booming or had almost tapped out. Nearly six months out of Missouri, and in average time despite their adversities, they arrived at the South Fork of California's American River. Hearst and his companions headed first for Diamond Springs, then to Hangtown and finally on to Jackass Gulch, where recent promising strikes had been made.

The entire winter's work resulted in only a meager standard of gold-camp living. Cora Older, George Hearst's biographer, reports that his mining fortune was "no tale of easy, sudden success. So little was his gain that sometimes he said Jackass Gulch was well-named." Hearst and his cousins abandoned their claim in the spring of 1851 when he "knew that he and the Clarks would never be millionaires by washing gold in that unyielding granite canyon. The dust simply wasn't there."[2]

For the next seven years George continued to stake claims throughout the northern California gold fields. Early in 1858 George's stepfather, Joseph Funk, sent news of George's Missouri properties and asked him to return home to visit his aging mother. Hearst responded in March of 1858 by sending $300 to his mother, writing, "My chances are pretty good to make money at present. . . . If the claim. . . holds out as it has so far, it is one of the good things that is sometimes found in California." As for his return, he wrote to his stepfather, "I would like to see you and mother. . . much better than you suppose, but to come home without money is out of the question; but if I have any kind of luck I will come home soon and stop awhile, though I do not expect to make [Missouri] my home; I am satisfied I could not stand that climate."[3]

As George continued to hunt for a fortune from the earth, life on the trail became natural to him. He prospected on the western slope of the Sierra until July of 1859, when the Comstock Lode was discovered near the present town of Carson City, Nevada. George Hearst and his friends traveled east over the Sierra on pack mules, part of the "great backward rush from California." Although the Comstock mining area had been prospected by eager gold miners for the past 10 years with some success, Hearst was one of the first to examine the "heavy black stuff" that clogged the mining pans and rockers. While the other miners believed that the black ore was lead and discarded it, Hearst thought it might be silver. He quickly staked a claim named the Ophir.

In March of 1860, almost 10 years after leaving Missouri, George Hearst realized $80,000 from his mine. He bought another claim, the Gould & Curry, to add to his original Ophir holdings. A new mining camp, Virginia City, sprang up as Hearst's and other miners' claims paid handsomely. Hearst invested a portion of his new fortune in other mines, banked another portion and then decided to make his long-awaited trip back to Missouri and his mother, so he could "see her have all that life could desire."[4] Once home, George found his mother "very low with consumption." He spent seven months at his mother's home, until Elizabeth Hearst Funk died on April 1, 1861.

During this period George, now nearing his forties, also took the time to reacquaint himself with his neighbors, including Phoebe Elizabeth Apperson, the 18-year-old daughter of Randolph Walker and Drucilla Whitmire Apperson. The Appersons were also a prosperous, slave-owning family with Virginia and South Carolina antecedents. Phoebe was born on the family farm in Franklin County, Missouri, on December 3, 1842.

According to George Hearst's biographer, ". . .Ph[o]ebe Elizabeth Apperson was mystical, different from the women he had seen in the past ten years; determined, rugged women of the prairie schooners; women of the fandango houses; women who could use a rocker like a man. Ph[o]ebe. . .was a vision. She had grace and charm and touches of humor like his own. Though she had been brought up in a log cabin she could play the piano. . . .She was eager to learn."[5]

Phoebe had been educated in the rural county school and received further schooling under a St. Louis governess, although her desire for a wider education was repeatedly noted by family and friends. Because George Hearst had received, at most, two years of formal education, his courtship of the intellectual Phoebe was not taken seriously by family or friends. When he continued to call upon her, Phoebe's parents objected to any match between them primarily because of the difference in their ages.

Cora Older states that George was "too modest" to tell Phoebe of his Nevada silver mine, but news of his prosperity had preceded him. The day before they eloped on June 15, 1862, to Steelville, Missouri, George Hearst and Phoebe Apperson entered into a prenuptial legal agreement. She agreed to marry George, who in turn conveyed 50 shares of Gould & Curry mining stock to Phoebe for "her exclusive use as long as she lived."[6]

Phoebe wearing formal dress.

In September of 1862 George Hearst left Missouri with his new bride and headed first to St. Louis and then on to New York City, where they boarded a steamer bound for the Isthmus of Panama and, ultimately, San Francisco. On shipboard, the Hearsts made the acquaintance of David and Margaret Peck and their two children, Orrin and Helen, who were also relocating to San Francisco. Seasickness and the early months of pregnancy gave Phoebe Hearst a most difficult passage.

Late in 1862 the Hearsts sailed through the Golden Gate, fortified in the event of Confederate attack at Black (now Fort) Point. In 1862, San Francisco had a population nearing 80,000, including "velvet-footed Chinese with long queues, wearing bright mandarin coats, Indians in blankets, Mexicans in sombreros, American dandies in silk hats and broadcloth, bearded miners, soft-voiced southern women and high-nosed executive New England women."[7]

To Phoebe, who had been raised in a rural area, the sights and sounds of this bustling city were fascinating. George and Phoebe Hearst first lived at the Lick House, the finest hotel in the city. Shortly after their arrival, they moved to the less ornate Stevenson House, which stood on the northwest corner of California and Montgomery Streets. Here Phoebe gave birth to her first and only child, William Randolph Hearst, on April 29, 1863.

Although Phoebe expressed her willingness to live with her husband in the mining camps, George thought San Francisco was the only respectable place for his wife and son. He decided to make trips back and forth between his family and the mines 200 miles away. A brick house on Rincon Hill, then a most fashionable address, became the Hearsts' new home.

As George became increasingly involved in his mining ventures, Phoebe devoted her time, attention, and intellect to nurturing her son. By many accounts, including his own, William Randolph Hearst was an indulged child. According to Hearst's principal biographer, W.A. Swanberg, "Willie was given just about every-thing he wanted, including a pony and a cart and a Punch and Judy show in the barn." His mother called him Willie; his father nicknamed him "Billy Buster." He was given two dogs, beginning a lifetime of affectionate regard for dogs and other animals he attempted to domesticate as pets.

Phoebe also turned her formidable energy to the task of winning a place in the society of mid-century San Francisco. As a frontier town, San Francisco had social standards based first on wealth and then on background and breeding. In this environment the newlywed Hearsts excelled, for George Hearst sought wealth as assiduously as Phoebe courted culture. Their child would inherit their determination for and love of both worlds in almost equal measure.

To prepare herself for the task of guiding young Willie's future education, Phoebe took private language lessons, visited art museums and galleries, and attended the opera and other musical events.

George began at this time to acquire large parcels of land throughout the West. Ranchland along the central California coast, including the original Mexican ranchos of Piedras Blancas, San Simeón, and Santa Rosa were among his first purchases. George continued to buy up surrounding parcels from willing or unwilling neighbors throughout his life.

In the summer of 1872 George Hearst traveled to Salt Lake City, Utah, to investigate some new business prospects. Miners with claims were eager to attract George Hearst's interest, for his reputation was high, his knowledge was sound and his movements were followed by other prospectors and investors as potential leads to new mining districts and rich claims. He made the 35-mile trip southeast of Salt Lake City to a mountainous canyon near the mining town of Park City. There he met with two Canadian miners who were discouraged by the hard work and long period of time they had invested in their claims with little tangible reward.

Hearst offered them $27,000 for the Ontario mine, as well as $3,000 to another man who claimed an interest. Hearst and his partner, James Ben Ali Haggin, jointly owned the mine.[8] For the first three years the account books were kept in red ink. Sizable amounts of capital were necessary to build rock crushers, mills, and smelters in the mountains near Parley's Peak. These expenditures greatly strained Hearst's financial resources.

Left: George Hearst (1820-91).
Below: George Hearst's Homestake Mine in South Dakota.

Phoebe and Willie remained in San Francisco. Her longing for artistic and cultural education could no longer be satisfied by trips to local galleries and literary gatherings of her friends. Only a Grand Tour of Europe, that status symbol of the rising Gilded Age, could satisfy Phoebe and her son.

Many preparations were made, including consulting Baedeker's guidebooks and retaining the services of a private tutor. In the early spring of 1873, just before Willie turned 10, Phoebe and her son set out for St. Louis on the first leg of their journey. They traveled swiftly on the four-year-old transcontinental railroad, a remarkable advance in comfort over George's hazardous overland journey little more than 20 years earlier.

Phoebe, with typical determination, decided to write to George in the form of a diary so complete that he would be able to share their experiences. They sailed for Great Britain on the *Adriatic* in April, 1873. The Hearst party's itinerary included Ireland, Scotland, England, Germany, Switzerland, France and Italy. As Swanberg points out, "For the average boy of ten, a year and a half in Europe would be a dreary eternity. . .[but] Willie Hearst was no average boy. He showed a keen interest in what he saw that saved him from boredom and showed a maturing intellect. He had a lively sense of pity. In Dublin he was troubled by the sight of overworked horses and by a depth of poverty he had never seen in America."[9]

The lessons that Phoebe planned with a private tutor coincided beautifully with their travels. Willie was

able to read about medieval Britain as they toured the lost keeps of England, Scotland, Wales and Ireland. Phoebe wrote that "Willie would have liked to live" at Windsor Castle, indicating a fascination for the historic site that would induce him to return many times throughout his life.[10] The German language and its folklore were studied as they sailed down the Rhine, stopping for tours of the *schlosses* that lined the banks.

Verona, Florence, Rome, and Venice provided powerful artistic images from the Renaissance that Hearst would one day rely upon when planning his estate at San Simeon. At one point in their travels, Willie appears to have exhausted even the redoubtable Phoebe, who confided in a letter to her husband she believed Willie "is getting a mania for travel, but I think we had best come home."[11]

During their lengthy stay in Florence, Phoebe "had difficulty convincing Willie there were other places to see & that we could not buy all we saw. He gets so fascinated his reason and judgment forsake him. I too acknowledge the temptation. . . ."[12]

The artistic sights prompted Willie to ask his mother for drawing lessons. She anxiously consulted George by mail:

> He is begging me to allow him to take drawing lessons, but I am afraid it would not be best to undertake so many things. He would do none well. . . .He is picture crazy. I do not mean to say he has any special talent and would not wish him an artist (unless a great one) but he frequently surprises me in his expressions concerning the best pictures. If he only learns to sketch enough to amuse & interest himself I should be glad.[13]

Phoebe remonstrated with George for his infrequent and very brief letters. When she left California, George's mining interests were in a precarious state because the Ontario mine required great infusions of capital. A national bank panic and an alarming depression in the economy had wrought havoc with the price of gold and silver, further complicating George's business affairs.

Left: George Hearst acquired large parcels of land on the Central California coast, as indicated in this letter from his attorney regarding land leases.

Below: The lighthouse near the Hearst property.

Despite the precarious state of the family finances, the Hearsts decided to complete their tour of Europe. After 18 months of travel, Phoebe and her son arrived back in New York City on October 23, 1874.

Upon their return to San Francisco, several drastic financial decisions were made. Strict economy was practiced until the future of the Ontario mine was no longer in doubt. They sold the Chestnut Street home and their horses and carriages, dismissed the servants and, most startling of all, placed Willie in public school for the first and only time in his life. According to Swanberg, Willie attended four different elementary schools in the coming year, which lends credence to young Hearst's reputation as a mischief-maker. He and his mother boarded with friends, while his father headed back to his Utah and Nevada mines.

The family's financial straits were eased when the Ontario mine began to pay in September of 1876. By the end of 1876, the firm of Hearst & Haggin had netted $1,100,000. From 1877 to George Hearst's death in 1891, the Ontario yielded $12,425,000, providing a bedrock for the Hearst fortune and George's continuing speculation in mines and real estate. On these proceeds, the Hearsts also resumed the good life, rehiring domestic help and private tutors, purchasing new teams and carriages, and buying an outsized house at 734 Sutter, another fashionable San Francisco address.

The Ontario mine also provided some of the capital for new mining ventures at Deadwood in the Black Hills of the Dakota Territory. George directed his agents to begin buying claims while he liquidated much of his family's holdings and secured additional financial backing from brokers in San Francisco. Hearst and Haggin also added another partner to their syndicate, Lloyd Tevis, president of Wells Fargo.[14] With this backing, Hearst hurried to Lead City, the largest of the mining boom towns, arriving in early July of 1877.

He already owned the original Homestake claim, a $70,000 purchase. George bought the adjoining Golden Terra claim for $35,000. He pursued 250 separate claims on 2,616 acres, combining them into one gigantic mining claim, which he still called the Homestake. Hearst wrote to his partner, Haggin, "I will hurt a good many people. And it is quite possible that I may get killed, but if I should I can't but lose a few years [he was 58], and all I ask of you is to see that my wife and child gets [sic] all that is due them from all the sources and that I am not buried in this place."[15]

"All the sources" to which Hearst referred included not just the vast and abundant Homestake mine, but also the Hearst Mercantile Company and the Hearst-owned reservoir and railroad. George Hearst's blind determination to control the Deadwood fields parallels the methods used by his contemporaries in business and industry, who used sharp dealings and shrewd manuevers to acquire vast wealth. Such single-minded tactics earned the label of "robber baron" for John D. Rockefeller in the oil fields of Pennsylvania, Andrew Carnegie in Pittsburgh steel production, Jay Gould and Cornelius Vanderbilt in Eastern railroads, and J.P. Morgan in banking.

This newest Hearst fortune made possible a move in 1878 to 726 California Street, where the family remained for the next four years. The success of the Ontario and the promise of the Homestake mine meant that Phoebe could take a second trip to Europe, which she had once feared she would never have. This tour would be remarkably similar to her first. Will, as he now preferred to be called, would naturally accompany her, and Thomas Barry was enlisted as the private tutor who provided lessons that complemented the surroundings.

As an addendum to one of Willie's letters to his father, Phoebe writes, "I have allowed Willie to write this without any assistance from me. Although the writing is bad, he can express himself moderately well. He reminds me of you in his aversion to writing, but if practice & perseverance can change him, I will try it."

Thomas Barry kept a diary of this period, from May to August of 1879, which documents a recurring streak of mischief in his charge. Barry reveals himself in the diary as an intensely serious young man who felt his obligations to educate the Hearst heir quite keenly.

Friday, June 6 . . .After Will's exercise we went to the Louvre and I showed Will the beautiful things in the statuary department - feasting myself again on Venus. Will prefers Vatican Venus - one with bronze sheath. . . .We worked from 4 to 6. After dinner I took a ride with Mrs. H. and then gave Will his usual lesson and then after reading some and writing some letters for Mrs. H. to her shipping agent in Liverpool and to bankers in London I went to bed after 11. . . .

Saturday, June 7. . .Started for Louvre after making Will study a half hour for morning transgressions. . . .

Wednesday, June 11. . .After Will's exercise—during which [he was] rude to [the riding] Master with idiotic attempts at fun which highly amused [a friend]—we then went to Pantheon—front like a Grecian temple.

. . .After dinner I went out riding with Mrs. H., Will and Eugene [Lent] to the Bois, which was very lovely. After returning at about 9 we celebrated the occasion with Champagne. . . .[16]

After nearly four months of travel and sightseeing, Phoebe Hearst decided to return to Germany at the close of the summer for an extended stay at a health spa, while Will returned to America in the company of Thomas Barry to enroll at St. Pauls, an Eastern prep school.

At school, Hearst was not only homesick and missed his mother, but he also hated the regimen and structure of prep school and the frigid, bleak New England winters that were a sharp contrast to the pleasant California climate. In the first months away from her, he flooded Phoebe with a stream of pitiful letters that he hoped would win his freedom:

. . .I am working very hard "nine hours per day" and even then can hardly keep up with the form. . . . .I feel very despondent and lonely all the time and wish for you to come awful bad.

It has been over a week since I recieved [sic] a letter, and I feel very anxious for fear you are sick. If you are I would much rather know. It is the next thing to speaking with you to write and recieve [sic] a letter.

It is all I can do to keep from crying sometimes when [I realize] how much alone I am and how far away you are. . .the only thing that comforts me is that the time is getting shorter every day till you will be here. . . .

It is very cold every morning. I have to wear heave [sic] under cloathing [sic] and a fall suit. . . . Do come home soon.[17]

His letters were effective, because after little more than a year Phoebe let him return to San Francisco and resume his studies with private tutors.

George was again away from home on mining business. In 1881, two years after he had consolidated his holdings in South Dakota and headed to a claim in Arizona, George Hearst heard of yet another fantastic strike. One of his agents told him of a silver mine on Anaconda Hill, near Butte, Montana. He telegraphed instructions to buy a 25 percent interest in this mine, sight unseen, even though it was commonly believed most of the silver and gold in this area had already been discovered during earlier strikes. Hearst left for Montana, carrying, as his son later recalled, suitcases full of ore samples.

The first samples from the Anaconda mine were promising for their copper content. Hearst ordered the installation of a smelter, purchased water rights and began operating a railroad into the district. From 1881 until George Hearst's death 10 years

Phoebe (center) rides an elephant during one of her trips abroad.

later, over 400 million pounds of copper were taken from the Anaconda.

The Hearst mining fortune, secure after the Ontario silver strikes, was made invincible by the Homestake and the Anaconda mines. George Hearst continued to roam the West, investigating mines and buying claims. He also made further investments in San Francisco real estate and purchased land surrounding his Piedras Blancas holdings. Occasionally he and his son traveled 200 miles south to the ranch to camp and to investigate the progress of the cattle ranching on the property.

In 1878 George directed the construction of a wharf on San Simeon Bay and a two-story house a short distance from the sea, making it possible for Phoebe to sail down the coast to visit the ranch for the first time since its purchase 13 years earlier.

George's political ambitions were growing apace with his wealth. He made substantial contributions to the Democratic Party and loans in excess of $100,000 to its foundering San Francisco newspaper, the *Examiner*. George became the newspaper's owner in October of 1880 in lieu of repayment of the loans. Although George was unenthusiastic about his newest acquisition, he did concede the importance of maintaining a newspaper that favored his party's efforts. However, the newspaper made no difference in his unsuccessful bid for the Democratic nomination for governor of California in 1882. Will first visited the *Examiner*'s offices during the period before he left for college, but no record remains of his initial impressions of journalism.

In the fall of 1882 Will traveled to Cambridge with his mother and enrolled at Harvard, then open only to male students. At 19, Hearst was tall, slender and good-looking, but his voice had not dropped to the lower registers that people expected from a young man of his build. He wore his hair parted precisely in the middle and slicked down with tonic, a style favored by nearly all of his fashionable peers. Given the clannish nature of his Eastern classmates, Will's circle of friends was drawn primarily from the "Cal boys," sons of his father's business partners. Eugene

William Randolph Hearst (right) with friend during his college days at Harvard.

Top: The Music room at Phoebe's Hacienda in Pleasanton, California.

Above: Originally built by Phoebe in Berkeley, California, Hearst Hall burned in 1922. Hearst had the gymnasium rebuilt in 1927 as a memorial to his mother.

Lent, a companion since childhood, and Jack Follansbee, an Oakland boy, were his closest friends. He followed college sports avidly and four university clubs counted on his congenial nature as well as his generosity.

In addition to the expert appreciation of the fine arts that his mother had spent nearly 20 years instilling, Will retained his fondness for pranks and jokes as well as a distaste for the regimented, scholastic life. The New England winters he abhorred in prep school continued to affect his disposition throughout his college years. When Will was depressed (which he termed the "dumps" or the "molly grubs"), he was sometimes able to mitigate the bad feelings by purchasing some *bibelot*, strolling through an art gallery, writing to his mother, or traveling to New York to attend the theater:

(Homesick for California)
Harvard University
Cambridge, Mass.

Dear Mother:—

. . .I feel very dismal. I had a cold for a few days and then (as I telegraphed) I had the pink eye. . . . I awake in the morning to find one or both of my eyes closed, and sometimes I am able to open them only by using my hands. . . . I have had to be very careful — stop

smoking altogether, stop reading, except in the early morning, and go to bed at the unreasonable hour of nine o'clock. . . .

There is but little going on here at present and what little there is doesn't interest me much. I have had the "molly grubs" for the last week or so. I am beginning to get awfully tired of this place and I long to get out West somewhere where I can stretch myself without coming in contact with the narrow walls with which the prejudice of the beaneaters has surrounded us. . . .

I long to see our own woods, the jagged rocks and towering mountains, the majestic pines, the grand impressive scenery of the "far West."

I shall never live anywhere but in California and I like to be away for awhile only to appreciate it the more when I return.

. . .Here I am almost busted again before the month is ended. For of the $50 that remained over from what you sent me after everything was paid, twelve dollars went immediately for photographs of my room and the rest has gradually leaked out until now I have only $10 to my name and what I am to do next month when my drug store and livery and my pink-eye doctor bills come in I don't know. Besides next month I will have to [have] tutor[ing] a little — I hope a very little — and this will take still more money and then there will be a farewell dinner or two. Oh, my, Harvard is no place for a poor boy.

. . .I know that I may have to work my way in the world and. . .I do not feel terrified at the prospect, although, of course, I should prefer to have enough money to be able to turn my time to politics or science or something where I could make a name. . . .[18]

An increasingly busy social life, on and off campus, did nothing to reconcile Hearst to the rigors of both the Harvard curriculum and Massachusetts winters. His scholastic status continued to slide, primarily because of his absence from the classroom rather than any difficulty with the courses. His increasing admiration for theater led him to join the Hasty Pudding Club. Of his acceptance into this group, he wrote, "I had a very pleasant time running for the club and didn't have to do anything but sing and dance and say my temperance speech. I met a great many nice fellows who treated me very kindly. . . ."[19]

Shortly after his senior year began, Hearst was brought up short by the Dean, who noted Will's chronic absence from the classroom and his failure to take several make-up tests. The bad news was sent to Phoebe by telegraph: "SAW THE DEAN, REQUESTED NOT TO RETURN. SAW THE PRESIDENT, SAID IF I WENT TO A GOOD CLIMATE AND STUDIED WITH A COMPETENT INSTRUCTOR, I SHOULD PROBABLY BE ALLOWED TO PASS MY EXAMINATIONS IN JUNE. SHALL I ENGAGE INSTRUCTION? WHAT SALARY ARE YOU WILLING TO PAY?"[20]

His mother hurried to the East Coast, ready to begin the now-familiar process of hiring tutors and planning a course of study that would reopen Harvard's doors to Will. When she arrived in Boston, she found a mutinous note from her son informing her that he had gone to New Haven for the Harvard-Yale baseball game and would return in a few days. "I assured the gentlemen of the Faculty of Harvard College," he wrote, "that I didn't regret so much having lost my degree as having given them an opportunity to refuse it to me." [21]

Clearly, Will was not disturbed by his suspension. His coursework had never inspired any sustained application of his intelligence. A fellow student summed up Hearst's attitude succinctly by noting he was a student of "amiable indolence broken by spasms of energy." [22] Perhaps the most significant "spasm of energy" was Hearst's stint as business manager of the Harvard *Lampoon* the previous spring.

The campus humor magazine had never been operated profitably, relying instead upon student staff members who were wealthy enough to make up any deficits out of their own pockets. Eugene Lent had originally been named to the post of business manager, but his allowance, unlike Hearst's, was not generous enough to meet the *Lampoon*'s finan-

A portrait of Phoebe Apperson Hearst by F. B. Johnstone.

cial needs. An offer was made to Hearst to co-manage the "sheet" with his friend, which he accepted. But instead of simply telegraphing home for additional funds from the seemingly bottomless Hearst fortune, he proposed to untangle the *Lampoon's* financial morass directly, running the magazine as a business.

Hearst and Lent drummed up advertising from Cambridge businesses and appealed to students and alumni to take subscriptions. Their strategy was overwhelmingly successful, putting the magazine in the black for the first time. Will wrote to Phoebe of his *coup,* "Show this to Papa and tell him just to wait till Gene and I get hold of the old *Examiner* and we'll boom her in the same way - she needs it." [23]

With his suspension, Hearst no longer had the *Lampoon* upon which to sharpen his journalistic instincts. He thought Washington was the ideal place to serve out his suspension, with "opportunities of hearing the debates in Congress, familiarizing myself with legislative methods of procedure, and thus at once assisting my present college studies and preparing the way for a brilliant entree into the political arena, some time in the future."

Hearst, who adopted the abbreviated form of address, W.R., in his waning college days, wrote to his father at the time of his suspension that he was considering a future career in "law, politics or journalism, and under favorable circumstances it might be possible to combine all three." [24] Although he attended to his tutors that winter, Will also found time to study the New York, Boston and Washington daily papers and to form strong opinions about what he found successful or wanting in each paper. The newspaper Hearst found himself drawn to was Joseph Pulitzer's New York *World,* a working-class publication that offered readers a mélange of news laced with scandal, gossip, and adventure.

In mid-March of 1886, George joined his wife and son in Washington. California Senator John Miller had died in office and George Hearst was appointed by Governor George Stoneman to fill the seat until a

replacement was elected on July 3, 1886. Phoebe found a suitably impressive house in the Capitol at 1400 New Hampshire Avenue, NW and began to recreate the successes of her San Francisco *salon.* She and Will also availed themselves of the cultural resources of the city. The new senator filled his days with politicking, despite his discomfort in the frock coat he was now compelled to wear. He particularly enjoyed the camaraderie of his fellow senator, railroad entrepreneur Leland Stanford.

Before his father arrived in Washington, Will wrote to him, this time expressing direct hopes for a journalistic career. His long, carefully worded letter reveals a capacity for detail that was missing from his academic work:

Dear Father:—

I have just finished and dispatched a letter to the Editor of the Examiner- *. . .comment[ing] on the illustrations, if you may call them such, which have lately disfigured the paper. . . .*

I [wrote] that in my opinion the cuts that have recently appeared in the paper bore an unquestionable resemblance to the Cuticura Soap advertisements; and I . . .believe that our editor has illustrated many of his articles from his stock on hand of cuts representing gentlemen before and after using that efficacious remedy.

. . .Let me beg of you to remonstrate with him and thus prevent him from giving the finishing stroke to our miserable little sheet. . . .I am convinced that I could run a newspaper successfully.

Now if you should make over to me the Examiner, — *with enough money to carry out my schemes, — I'll tell you what I would do.*

In the first place I would change the general appearance of the paper and make seven wide columns where we now have nine narrow ones, then I would have the type spaced more, and these two changes would give the pages a much cleaner and neater appearance.

Below: Phoebe's Hacienda del Pozo de Verona before it was remodeled by Hearst Castle architect, Julia Morgan.
Top right: Garden at the Hacienda del Pozo de Verona with the pink Verona marble wellhead found by the Hearsts on one of their European trips. The wellhead was later moved to San Simeon.
Bottom right: Julia Morgan's plans for the new Hacienda.

SCALE EIGHT FEET TO ONE INCH · H A C I E N D A   D E L   P A Z O   D E L   V E R O N A · ELEVATION SCHEME B

Secondly, it would be well to make the paper as far as possible original. . .and to imitate only some such leading journal as the New York World *which is undoubtedly the best paper of that class to which the* Examiner *belongs, —that class which appeals to the people and which depends for its success upon enterprise, energy and a certain startling originality and not upon the wisdom of its political opinions or the lofty style of its editorials. . . .*

Thirdly, we must advertise the paper from Oregon to New Mexico and must also increase our number of advertisements [even] if we have to lower our rates to do it. . . .

Illustrations embellish a page; illustrations attract the eye and stimulate the imagination of the lower classes and materially aid the comprehension of an unaccustomed reader and thus are of particular importance to that class of people which the Examiner *claims to address. . . .*

And now to close with a suggestion of great consequences, namely, that all these changes be made not by degrees but at once so that the improvement will be very marked and noticeable and will attract universal attention and comment. . . .

Well goodbye. I have given up all hope of having you write to me, so I suppose I must just scratch along and trust to hearing of you through the

newspapers. By the way, I heard you had bought 2000 acres of land the other day and I hope some of it was the land adjoining our ranche [sic] that I begged you to buy in my last letter.[25]

In this letter he makes plain his desire to pursue a journalistic career, but it seems everyone in the family had conflicting ideas about what path William Randolph Hearst should take. His mother continued to opt for higher education, while George hoped to interest him in the management of the family's land and mining properties. Even his maternal grandfather, Randolph Apperson, had his opinions about Will's future, writing to a relative, "Our Grandboy, Willie Randolph Hearst has graduated & come home. He is 22 years of age & very boyish at that but he is going right to work assisting his father. I trust this will make a man of him. His father has a large stock ranch in waiting for him, so you see if there is any work in him he will have plenty to keep him out of mischief."[26]

Instead of immediately adopting the ranching life, Will began a series of trips with Jack Follansbee at his father's request to visit various Hearst-owned enterprises. Swanberg believes that Will was also able to spend some time in New York City, working on the newspaper he most admired, Joseph Pulitzer's *World*. Other biographers believe that Hearst returned to Har-

vard during this period, though he did not take his degree. Records detailing his activities during this year are varied, but it is evident that William Randolph Hearst matured appreciably. Instead of the letters from college that rationalized his poor attendance record and poorer marks, Hearst began to send (especially to his father) letters that reveal his organizational skills and shrewd grasp of situations.

George was elected in his own right to a six-year term in the Senate, beginning in March of 1887. Despite the variety of activities in the year past, Will retained his original enthusiasm for the newspaper business in general and the San Francisco *Examiner* in particular. George was still unconvinced that journalism was a suitable career, but he relented and deeded ownership of the newspaper to his son.

On the same day George Hearst was sworn into office as a United States senator from California, his son began a 65-year career in journalism with an inconspicuous announcement on an inside page of the March 4, 1887 issue of the San Francisco paper: "The *Examiner*, with this issue, has become the exclusive property of William R. Hearst, son of its former proprietor. It will be conducted in future on the same lines and policies which characterized its career under the control of Senator Hearst."[27]

Part One Endnotes

1 *Franklin County Tribune*, Union, Missouri, November 24, 1899, quoted in Ralph Gregory, "George Hearst in Missouri," *Missouri Historical Society Bulletin*, 21 (1965) 77.

2 Cora Older, *George Hearst, Pioneer* (Los Angeles: Westernlore, 1966) 84.

3 George Hearst (GH) to Joseph Funk, March 18, 1858, quoted in Gregory 62.

4 Gregory 62.

5 Older 113.

6 Crawford County [Missouri] Marriage Contracts, Book A, Nos. 1, 4, 5.

7 Older 120.

8 James Ben Ali Haggin (1821-1914) was born into a prominent Kentucky family. (His exotic name derives from his maternal grandfather, who was a Turkish physician.) Haggin went to Sacramento in 1850 where he practiced law with Milton S. Latham. Haggin and his brother-in-law, Lloyd Tevis, moved their land and brokerage business to San Francisco in 1853 and eventually began a long association with George Hearst. See the Older Collection of manuscript and research materials on George Hearst, Special Collections, California Polytechnic State University.

9 W.A. Swanberg, *Citizen Hearst* (New York: Scribners, 1961) 14.

10 Phoebe A. Hearst (PAH) to GH, June 15, 1873, PAH Papers, Bancroft.

11 PAH to GH, December 15, 1873, PAH Papers, Bancroft.

12 PAH to GH, October 5, 1873, PAH Papers, Bancroft.

13 PAH to GH, December 3, 1873, PAH Papers, Bancroft.

14 Lloyd Tevis (1824-1899) moved to California in 1849 from his native Kentucky. After an unsuccessful stint as a prospector, he opened a land

office in Sacramento with his brother-in-law, James Haggin. He moved to San Francisco in 1853 to practice law with the firm of Crockett, Page and Tevis, but "his brokerage business with J.B. Haggin soon absorbed the major share of his attention." From the Older Collection, Cal Poly.

15 GH to James Haggin, undated, quoted in Michael Cieply, "The Loded Hearst," *Westways* 73.6 (1965) 78.

16 All Barry passages taken from ts. Thomas Barry Diary, The Bancroft Library.

17 William Randolph Hearst (WRH) to PAH, [Autumn, 1879], PAH Papers, Bancroft.

18 WRH to GH, [Autumn, 1884], WRH Papers, Bancroft.

19 WRH to GH, 1885, WRH Papers, Bancroft.

20 WRH to PAH, October 4, 1885, PAH Papers, Bancroft.

21 WRH to GH, November 23, 1885, WRH Papers, Bancroft.

22 *Collier's*, September 22, 1906.

23 WRH to GH, [Spring, 1885], WRH Papers, Bancroft.

24 WRH to GH, both passages from November 23, 1885, WRH Papers, Bancroft.

25 WRH to GH, [c. 1885], WRH Papers, Bancroft.

26 Randolph Apperson to Lucy Walker, August 12, 1886, HF Papers, Bancroft. Apparently Hearst's grandfather was not aware that Will had left the university without his degree. He also mistakenly gives William Randolph Hearst's age as 22 when he actually had turned 23 the previous April.

27 San Francisco *Examiner*, March 4, 1887.

Phoebe Apperson Hearst and William Randolph Hearst at the Pleasanton Hacienda.

THE WORLD OF JOURNALISM

William Randolph Hearst arrived on the journalistic scene at a time of unprecedented change. During the period from 1880 to 1890, newspapers serving large urban areas were growing at a phenomenal pace, partly because Americans were moving in record numbers from rural areas to cities. Increasing numbers of European immigrants also contributed to the booming urban population.

The proliferation of newspapers also owed a great deal to recent technological advances. Newspapers reached their destinations more quickly because of improved transportation. News gathering was aided immeasurably by the use of the telephone, the telegraph and the beginning of wire services that provided dispatches from remote locations. Newsprint was manufactured more rapidly and at less expense with the advent of wood pulp papermaking processes. High-speed printing was made possible by multipage presses and Linotype.

But the greatest change at the time William Randolph Hearst entered the field was in the *people* who read newspapers. For the individual who had moved from the farm to the city or arrived from a foreign country, "the daily newspaper was the chronicler of the national scene and interpreter of the new environment." [1]

Two more critical factors explain the growth in newspapers during this period. The literacy rate doubled in the last 30 years of the 19th century, while the workweek declined by nearly 10 hours between 1850 and 1900. This increase in leisure time spurred the growth of newspapers and created the demand for new methods of entertainment and communications, such as national magazines, and later, motion pictures and newsreels. William Randolph Hearst eventually expanded his newspaper publishing empire to become involved in all three.

Joseph Pulitzer's New York *World*, which had fueled Hearst's interest in the business, was a model of the new urban newspaper with a large and growing circulation. The articles published had entertainment value as well as news content. They not only commanded attention, they were also easy to read and low-priced. The results of investigative reporting and crusades that championed the working classes were given prominent space. [2]

Though regarded as such by both friends and enemies, William Randolph Hearst was not a journalistic

THE OWNERSHIP OF THE "EXAMINER."

The EXAMINER, with this issue, has become the exclusive property of William R. Hearst, the son of its former proprietor. It will be conducted in future on the same lines and policies which characterized its career under the control of Senator Hearst.

Left: Sketch of William Randolph Hearst, proprietor of the New York Journal *and San Francisco* Examiner.

Above: This inconspicuous announcement in the March 4, 1887, issue of the Examiner *marked the beginning of Hearst's 65-year career in journalism.*

innovator. Rather, Hearst's genius lay in adapting the innovations of others to his own ends. The original ideas he copied in his newspapers were skill-fully molded and fitted to his pur-poses. His only innovation, and it was a considerable one, lay in the fact that he could take a new idea and put it into practice in a bigger and better way than the originator had ever conceived.

Hearst's early editorials for the *Examiner* began a long and unceasing tradition of Hearst publications prais-ing themselves. Although Will had been considered a convivial fellow at Harvard, he was also thought to be quite shy. This personal reticence was never carried over to the newspapers or other holdings that became a part of the Hearst empire. The *Examiner* was self-christened "Monarch of the Dailies," to which was later added the all-embracing, "Supreme in Everything."

Fueled by prodigious amounts of his time and his family's money, the newspaper began to attract attention and slowly build circulation. Early in 1887 Hearst wrote to his mother of his absorption in his new career:

. . .I don't suppose I will live more than two or three weeks if this strain keeps up. I don't get to bed until about two o'clock and I wake up at about seven in the morning and can't get to sleep again, for I must see the paper and compare it with the Chronicle. *If we are the best I can turn over and go to sleep with quiet satisfaction but if the* Chronicle *happens to scoop us, that lets me out of all sleep for the day.*

The newspaper business is no fun and I had no idea quite how hard a job I was undertaking when I entered upon the editorial management of the Exam-iner. . . . *The. . .great and good people of California want the* Examiner. *They*

don't want it very bad; they don't want it much harder than at the rate of about thirty additional copies a day, but. . .if we can manage to keep ahead we will have in a year from thirty to thirty-two thousand subscribers. That will put us away ahead of the Call *and well up with the* Chronicle.[3]

Hearst turned his attention to the equipment used to produce the paper, which consisted of an antiquated web press and two telephones housed in a rented building. Before the year was out, he was scouring the country, vis-iting newspaper offices to inspect their presses and appraise their staff. He sent his father a barrage of letters, broadly hinting at the need to pur-chase the most sophisticated 12-page presses.

In 1887 the *Chronicle*'s owner, M.H. de Young, decided to build a large new building for his newspaper's operation. Once Hearst heard of the plan, he was unsatisfied with the *Examiner*'s plebian rented building. He began an immediate letter campaign to his father for a permanent *Examiner* building. Hearst argued:

. . .Whether or not we like Mr. de Young's building, it is considered remarkably fine by everybody here. . . He is going to put in his tower the largest clock face in the world. . . .

These clock faces will front to the four points of the compass. . .and will be visible all over San Francisco and from Oakland. I didn't believe this. . .but I went across the bay and found that it was so. The tower can be seen distinctly now and when it is all lit [sic] up with electricity it will be simply tremendous. The entrances. . . will be finished in white marble and when these too are lit [sic] up with electricity it will be pretty dazzling. . . .

[The Chronicle building] will be the most substantial structure in town. This kind of thing has its effect on everybody. . . .It had an effect on Grandpa [Apperson] even. He said, "Dear me, that fellow must make an awful lot of money." He had heard all about de Young's building and he doesn't take the Chronicle. . . .

Of course friends of ours say the Examiner is going to put up a building too but they can't be saying that [forever]. . . .Now we are losing subscribers, we are losing advertisements, we are losing prestige. . . .

. . .You will have to do just as de Young has done. . . .You have got to put a million. . .or two million dollars into it. . . .[4]

Left: Front page of The Daily Examiner *the day Hearst took over its proprietorship from his father.*

Above: The Examiner *newsroom.*

The *Examiner* building did not become a reality for nearly six years, but it underscored his conviction that he must always outdo his competitors.

Hearst began to seek a new managing editor for the *Examiner*, hoping to find someone who shared his fervid vision of journalism and would be able to handle the day-to-day business of guiding the other editors and staff members. His search for a managing editor eventually ended on the East Coast when he met Sam Chamberlain, "a tall, urbane individual, a veteran newspaper reporter whose bouts with the bottle were widely spaced but determined." [5]

Another important addition to Hearst's staff was editorialist Arthur McEwen, who is often quoted for his succinct summation of the Hearst style: "What we're after is the 'Gee-whiz' emotion. We run our paper so that when the reader opens it, he says: 'Gee-whiz!'" [6] Within the privacy of the newsroom, McEwen elaborated on his journalistic philosophy. "Gee-whiz" was the reaction McEwen wanted from readers on the first page. The second page McEwen thought readers should cry, "Holy Moses!" and by the third page they should leap from their chairs, shouting, "God Almighty!" [7]

Writers who had already achieved recognition were also sought by Hearst, who prized their talent as well as their name value. Ambrose Bierce, the first acquisition, recalled their initial meeting vividly. Bierce was at work in his office at the San Francisco *Argonaut*, when he was interrupted by a young man:

> *"I am from the San Francisco* Examiner," *[Hearst] explained in a voice like the fragrance of violets made audible, and backed a little away.*
> *"Oh," I said, "you come from Mr. Hearst?" Then that unearthly child lifted his blue eyes and cooed, "I am Mr. Hearst."* [8]

A munificent salary induced Bierce to join the *Examiner*, where his barbed pen was used for commenting upon the events of the day in columns and features. He joined a number of crusades launched by Hearst, from reduced water rates in San Francisco to American intervention in Cuba, and the attempt to "bust the railroad trust."

Hearst was impressed with Bierce, who would remain with Hearst newspapers for 20 years, though he resigned and was immediately rehired with almost clockwork regularity. Bierce delivered scathing judgments on virtually any topic in his Sunday column, "The Passing Show: A Record of Personal Opinion and Dissent." Bierce's "personal opinion" kept Hearst's lawyers well-occupied on libel suits.

Hearst's generous salary offers induced other California writers, including Mark Twain, Gertrude Atherton, Bret Harte, Joaquin Miller and Jack London to join his staff. Winifred Black Bonfils, one of the first "sob sister" reporters, began her career in 1889 as a $15-per-week reporter for Hearst's paper. She was pigeonholed for a time by editors who felt the only topics suitable for women reporters were society parties and charity bazaars. As her assignments diversified, Bonfils began to use "Annie Laurie" as her pseudonym. She became a regular contributor to the *Examiner*, combining two facets of journalism well respected by Hearst: "created" news and the exposé. Editor Sam Chamberlain chose medical

treatment of the indigent as her first assignment.

Laurie had her doctor place belladonna drops in her eyes to achieve an authentic glaze. Dressed in shabby clothes with job advertisements stuffed in her pockets, she walked up and down Kearny Street several times before collapsing on the pavement. Her faint attracted a crowd of concerned San Franciscans, who summoned police. The officers assumed she was drunk and unceremoniously shoved her aboard an unsprung police wagon for a jolting ride to the city hospital. The doctor on duty administered an emetic by force and quickly turned her back onto the street.

Laurie's rousing account of her treatment in the next day's *Examiner* brought the suspension of the doctor, the re-evaluation of the hospital staff and the purchase of the city's first ambulance. The article also brought the guilty physician to the *Examiner*'s offices in a towering rage. According to the next day's paper (for this event was duly reported as well), during the ensuing fight a reporter landed a punch on the doctor, who "lay on his back whining like a whipped cur." [9]

Subsequent stories filed by Annie Laurie documented her experiences posing as a Mormon in polygamous Utah, a Salvation Army lassie on the vice-ridden Barbary Coast, a low-paid seasonal worker at an abusive fruit cannery, a naive consumer of quack cures and unsafe cosmetics, and an unskilled laborer at an exploitative cotton mill in the South. She also covered such diverse subjects as the leper colony on Molokai ("the saddest place on earth"), a prizefight, a whorehouse, and the overcrowded Children's Hospital in San Francisco.

The Hearst technique of arousing public sympathy with a mixture of sentiment and idealism proved to be a tremendous circulation booster when practiced by reporters of either gender. Male reporters did not write under pseudonyms, but they did undertake similar adventures in "created" news.

Ambrose Bierce and eight other *Examiner* writers were not content with merely reporting the story of two fisherman who had capsized outside the Golden Gate on a stormy evening. Instead they rented an oceangoing tug at the paper's expense, effecting a dramatic rescue. Hearst's joy was unalloyed, for the *Examiner* "came out an hour or so later with pictures, and a full account of the exploit, spread all over the first page. . . .The other papers appeared with a dismal story of how the ill-fated fishermen had been abandoned as lost." [10]

Well into his second year of publishing, Hearst showed no signs of disenchantment with his chosen profession. He kept his father and mother, who had both made substantial financial contributions, apprised of the progress of the paper. Hearst also constantly appealed to his father to use his influence on the *Examiner's* behalf, seizing every tool available to insure the success of his newspaper:

> . . .*Papa you must do your best for us and you must do it immediately. Delay would be as fatal as neglect.*

If we can get Senator Stanford to take an interest in the prosperity of our paper the greatest stroke towards its success will have been made.

At present the news companies on the trains — especially the S.P. — discriminate against the Examiner *for the benefit of the* Chronicle. . . .*We receive letters constantly saying that they can't get* Examiners *on the train and coming home I had a conversation with one of the news boys on the train and he said that the news company only gave him fifteen* Examiners *but that he could sell fifty.* [11]

Left: The present Examiner *building at 3rd & Market streets in San Francisco.*
Below: The original Examiner *building.*

Hearst conferring with Missouri senator, James A. Reed.

So blind was Hearst's determination to succeed that he ignored the difficult position in which he placed his father, asking him to gain Leland Stanford's support for a paper that relentlessly criticized Stanford's own railroad, the Southern Pacific.

Hearst was also blind to the amount of money he was constantly drawing upon for his newspaper's growth and development. Phoebe, however, had kept track of the figures, sending the following summary to George on August 7, 1888: "From Aug /87 to Aug /88 Will has spent *forty seven thousand*—nine *hundred and thirty-nine dollars*. This is *his* [personal] account, then the amount drawn for the *Examiner* is *one hundred & eighty* four thousand five hundred & *thirteen dollars*, making a very large sum." [12 *italics* original] Late in 1888 the Hearsts came to a joint decision

that their liberal financial support of the *Examiner* must stop.

When Will asked for an additional $50,000, both of his parents refused, disappointed that their son could not practice economic restraint, even though they had never taught it. Hearst was desperate, believing that he would lose the paper after nearly two years of constant labor. He appealed to Michael Francis Tarpey, the Democratic National Committee Chair from California, who also happened to be an old friend of George's from the early days of the gold rush. Tarpey reassured Will that the funds would be forthcoming from his father. "We were in the heat of a campaign," Tarpey recalled. "I went to the Senator and told him that the party needed contributions, and he was down for one hundred thousand dollars for the Democratic cause. The Senator didn't hesitate. I received his check for that amount. Half of the sum went into our campaign fund. The other fifty thousand dollars I turned over to young William for his and the paper's espousal of the Democratic principles. I do not know that Will ever required any more money for his paper. It soon became an outstanding and successful journal."[13]

It is likely that George Hearst relented and continued to help the *Examiner* directly, for the newspaper was not solvent until 1890. As George's health declined, he became increasingly concerned about the profligate amounts his son spent on the newspaper and on art objects.

On February 28, 1891, George Hearst died in his Washington, D.C., residence with Phoebe, Will, Jack Follansbee, and his physician at his bedside. The *New York Times* devoted two columns to his death, headlined:

DEATH OF SENATOR HEARST
END OF A CAREER WHICH WAS
PHENOMENAL.
FROM AN ILLITERATE PENNILESS
GOLDHUNTER TO A POPULAR
MEMBER OF THE NATIONAL
LEGISLATURE AND A
MILLIONAIRE.

The San Francisco *Examiner* devoted the whole front page, bordered in black, to the Senator's career. George Hearst left his entire estate, which included 18 million dollars, to his wife. The will continued to make William Randolph Hearst dependent upon his family to finance his business and personal life. It was also deeply wounding to Will that his father so obviously refused to trust his judgment about money. For the next three years Will practiced his version of economy, which included another trip to Europe and the long-awaited construction of a Hearst building to house the *Examiner*. In 1893, after the move into the new building was completed, Will wrote a straightforward letter to his mother, requesting a change in the handling of financial matters that would finally recognize him, at the age of 30, as an adult:

The Examiner's *fleet of automobiles, parked in front of the newspaper's temporary headquarters near the waterfront, following the fire of 1906.*

The request I make would not amount to an increase of my salary *so much as a* change of the manner of delivering it. *I beg of you to instruct Mr. Stump [the Hearst family's financial manager] to put to my credit at any bank on the first of each month a definite sum of $2500.*

. . .First, I think I might properly have now what was doubtless too much for me three years ago.

Secondly, I should be very happy to be relieved of the inconvenience of dealing with Stump. . . . As long as I come to ask him for extra thousand dollars here and there, he will treat me as a child asking ten cents for soda water. "Can't you get along with five cents?" "Soda water isn't very good for you anyhow." "Well come around next month and I will talk to you about it."

. . .Now positively *I* will, *from the moment this new arrangement goes into effect, lay aside, not to spend but to invest* one half *of all income from the paper, the ranch and all property that I may have or acquire.*

. . .I shall feel satisfied with [this] arrangement and will not demand or desire any *extra money. I will not be asking you for a thousand dollars on Christmas or a thousand on my birthday. . .[or] a thousand now and then for unforeseen expenses. . . . [14]*

Phoebe decided to sell her shares in the Anaconda mines, and from the proceeds, conferred $7.5 million on her son. While he was never able to manage his finances as he promised in the letter to his mother, he had secured a measure of financial independence. Without hesitation, he decided to corner the journalistic market in New York City. To achieve this goal it was necessary to compete directly with Joseph Pulitzer's *World*, the paper that had not only sparked his interest in publishing, but also provided the model for his success in San Francisco. The New York paper Hearst chose to buy was John McLean's *Journal*, although he did not publicly announce ownership of the paper until November 8 of that year.

One of Hearst's first moves was to drop the price to a penny an issue while expanding the paper to 16 sheets, a feat that would have been fiscally impossible without the Hearst fortune behind him. Pulitzer was unconcerned, for his paper had a large circulation, with morning, evening and Sunday editions selling at two cents apiece and advertising revenue far outstripping that of the nearly moribund *Journal*.

In less than six months Pulitzer was forced to pay attention to the Western newcomer at the *Journal*, as Hearst was using the well-proven methods of the new urban journalism. The working classes were courted with scare headlines on sensational news stories, an abundance of easy-to-read features, "created" news and exposés, and the Hearst self-publicizing policy.

Despite his precarious health, Pulitzer was a self-made man whose fortune came from journalism. He was said to have entered his New York newspaper building only once, preferring to do his business by telegraph and correspondence. The telegraphic messages were often relayed in code to foil spies in the publishing industry who Pulitzer was convinced were monitoring his moves. Hearst's code name became the word "Gush," reflecting Pulitzer's opinion of the amount of money Hearst spent advancing the *Journal*.

A sob sister was immediately hired for the New York paper. The writing style of this genre soon reached its florid peak, when the following story was filed by a Hearst reporter on a coal mine disaster:

I sobbed my way through the line of [bystanders who] stood aside to let me pass with a muttered, "The lady is from the Journal; *let her by." I was the first to reach the wounded and the dying. "God bless Mr. Hearst," cried a little child as I stooped to lave her brow; and then she smiled and died. I spread one of our comic supplements over the pale, still face and went on to distribute Mr. Hearst's generous bounty.*[15]

In addition to improving upon the gimmicks first used in the *World*, Hearst raided the staff of the rival

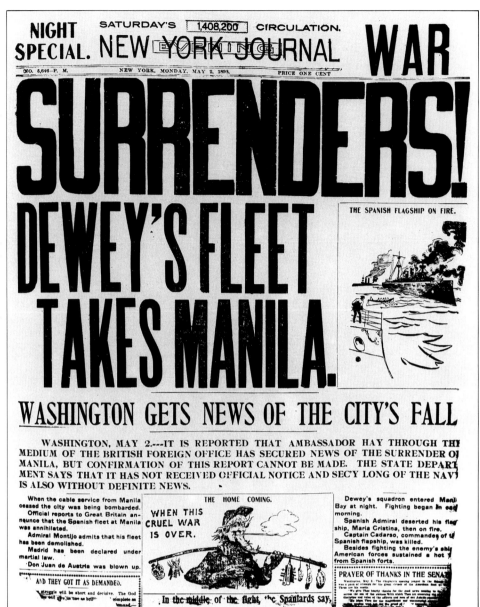

An ongoing rivalry existed between Hearst, owner of the Journal, *and* World *owner, Joseph Pulitzer. Hearst eventually succeeded in winning over Pulitzer's employees; and under former* World *employee Merrill Goddard's expert direction, introduced a Sunday supplement entitled* American Weekly.

paper, luring them with the now legendary Hearst-sized salaries. Editor Bill Nye wrote a friend, "I am leaving the *World,* at an advance of 50 percent on salary, by cracky, and going to the *Journal. . .".[16]

Merrill Goddard, who began working for Pulitzer in 1885 after graduating from Dartmouth, was renowned among New York journalists as the creator of the Sunday supplement. Under Goddard's editorship, the supplement grew in size and importance. Its content was created by a writer who "revamp[ed] the sensations of the week's news in nervous, bawling paragraphs." [17] Articles brimming with scandal, crime, and sex were prominently placed next to features on bizarre "scientific" discoveries.

In January of 1896, Hearst lured not only Goddard, the jewel in Pulitzer's crown, but also Goddard's entire staff to the *Journal.* Pulitzer made an immediate counteroffer, which restored his Sunday supplement staff, but only for one day. "Gush" trumped his rival's offer, finally winning Goddard, his staff, and a ready-made Sunday supplement.

Hearst's Sunday supplement, eventually entitled the *American Weekly,* reached its sensationalist zenith during Goddard's years at the *Journal.* Readers whiling away a Sunday afternoon reading the supplement were treated to headlines such as these:

CUTTING A HOLE IN A MAN'S CHEST TO LOOK AT HIS INTESTINES AND LEAVING A FLAP THAT WORKS AS IF ON A HINGE

THE SUICIDE OF A HORSE

SCIENCE CAN WASH YOUR HEART

Outcault surrounded by a variety of his cartoon characters.

Hearst also induced Richard Felton Outcault, the artist who is credited as the first Sunday newspaper cartoonist, to leave the *World*. In 1889, Pulitzer's paper had published Outcault's first Sunday "funny side," which consisted of a full newspaper page with the text of a short story describing the events in a single large colored drawing below it.

In 1895 Outcault created "Hogan's Alley," a serial "funny side," that included a background character named Johnny Dugan, an immigrant youngster with a bald head, outsized ears, and large feet. On Sundays, Dugan was always dressed in a yellow nightshirt, which "stood out like a sunrise" on the newspaper page. Johnny Dugan's popular name was born and soon New York went wild over the Yellow Kid.

As other New York publishers were scrambling to capitalize on the idea of the funny side, Outcault drew the Yellow Kid packing his bags and departing "Hogan's Alley" for "McFadden's Row of Flats," his new Hearst home. The term "yellow journalism" came into popular use at this time, symbolizing the sensational tactics Hearst, Pulitzer, and other publishers used in their war for the readership of New York City.

The Yellow Kid's "abnormal impishness" was succeeded seven years later by the pranks of an even more popular Outcault cartoon figure. Buster Brown, an upper-middle-class child, was accompanied on his cartoon adventures by his faithful dog, Tige, and less frequently, by his girlfriend, Mary Jane.

Left without Outcault's services, Pulitzer and other New York publishers decided to hire new cartoonists to draw ersatz Buster Browns and Yellow Kids for their newspapers. Soon genuine and imitation Outcault comic strips abounded in the pages of the *World*, the *Journal*, and the *Herald*. Suits and countersuits for copyright infringement were filed, occupying lawyers and judges for years to come.

Hearst's concern that readers would be confused by the imitators led him to run interviews with the cartoon characters in the news section of the *Journal*, under Hearst-inspired headlines:

BUSTER GOES OVER TO HEARST.

. . .COPYRIGHT SUITS IN SIGHT ON ACCOUNT OF TOW-HEADED YOUNGSTER.

FRIENDS HOPE HE WILL BE GOOD IN COURT. . .[18]

Hearst's method of reviewing the content of his own newspapers was quite unorthodox. Harry J. Coleman, who began as a copy boy and rose to the ranks of Hearst executives, described the first time he made a delivery to Hearst's office:

Hearst suddenly spread the proofs in precise order upon the floor and began a sort of tap dance around and between them. It was a mild, uncostumed combination of Carmen Miranda, a rumba, a Russian dagger dance and the Notre Dame shift, with lively castanet accompaniments produced by his snapping fingers. . . . The cadence of it speeded up in tempo [when he was displeased] and slowed down to a strolling rhythm when he approved. Between dances, he scribbled illegible scrawls in longhand on the margins. . . . [19]

Willis Abbot, one employee who had not previously worked for Pulitzer, served as New York editor-in-chief and was nominally responsible for the editorial page. In fact, Abbot, like Chamberlain in San Francisco, had been hired to provide day-to-day continuity. Hearst himself kept careful vigil over the editorials. Abbot recalled:

[Hearst's] greatest joy in life was to attend the theater, follow it up with a lively supper and, at about 1:30 a.m., turn up at the office full of scintillating ideas and therewith rip my editorial page to pieces. . . .It was always an interesting spectacle to me to watch this young millionaire, usually in irreproachable evening dress, working over the forms, changing a head here, shifting the position of an article there, clamoring always for more pictures and bigger type. [20]

Hearst signed a contract with R. F. Outcault by which Outcault's comics would appear in newspapers owned and operated by Hearst. Outcault's impish characters, Buster Brown and the Yellow Kid, appeared in cartoons such as the three pictured here.

Hearst summed up his journalistic philosophy in an editorial published one year after he began publishing his New York paper:

What is the explanation of the Journal's *amazing and wholly unmatched progress? . . .The* Journal *realized that which is frequently forgotten in journalism, that if news is wanted it often has to be sent for. . . .*

. . .It is the Journal's *policy to engage brains as well as to get the news, for the public is even more fond of entertainment than it is of information. . . .* [21]

Hearst was equally honest about his attitude toward the term "yellow journalism," which other publishers grew to believe was derogatory. Hearst used the term relentlessly in both of his newspapers, priding himself in practice of "Yellow journalism that yells." [22]

The power of yellow journalism is perhaps best illustrated by America's intervention in the Cuban revolution. Though Hearst is commonly associated with the events that led to the Spanish-American War, the role of Joseph Pulitzer, his very yellow *World,* and the combined circulation battle between them seldom receives equal attention.

The two newspapers were virtually tied in circulation. Pulitzer believed Hearst would spend himself out of business; Hearst believed Pulitzer's precarious nervous state would force him out of competition. "This was the situation," according to W.A. Swanberg, biographer of both men, "as the nation's two largest newspaper publishers brought up their siege guns in an attempt to exterminate each other by the cunning use of news. By pure chance it happened that the first big, continuous news issue that came to hand was the revolution in Cuba." [23]

Thus, the journalistic battle between Hearst and Pulitzer for the hearts and minds of New York newspaper readers erupted into a full-scale war in Cuba. The revolution in Cuba was of little concern to most Americans, but the power of the press brought the conflict home, presenting the rebels as machete-armed patriots in the tradition of Washington and Jefferson.

In the months before American intervention, the *Journal,* the *World,* and the yellow papers "stirred the country to a war psychosis, by not only reporting the events in Cuba, but [also] by making the news." [24] Hearst's reporters freed a Cuban nationalist jailed for trying to save her father's life. Later, the same reporters stole documents from a Spanish diplomatic pouch, and published one of the letters maligning President McKinley. The newspaper also offered a $50,000 reward for information about the sinking of the U.S.S. *Maine,* and sent an even larger contingent of reporters to Havana to investigate the cause of the explosion.

When war was officially declared in April of 1898, Hearst himself led a group of 20 reporters, including Jack Follansbee, to the front. Hearst filed his own dispatches, covering the Rough Riders' charge up San Juan Hill, the capture of Santiago and other war news. To his mother, who was concerned for his safety, he wrote: "I am at the front and absolutely safe, so don't worry. . . .[General Garcia] said the *Journal* had been the most potent influence in bringing the United States to the help of Cuba and they would always remember the *Journal* as a friend when friends had been very few. . . .Other [newspaper] proprietors are safely at home—and I will be soon. [25]

The circulation of both Hearst papers increased dramatically. Every aspect of the actual conflict, as well as a multitude of "created news" events, were reported in detail during the four-month war, which sometimes led to the publication of 40 extras in a single day. [26] Hearst returned to New York unharmed, his exploits the subject of a rare pro-Hearst editorial in the *New York Times:*

> *The editor and proprietor of the* Journal *of this city showed more than usually good judgment when he assigned Mr. W.R. Hearst to duty as a staff correspondent. . . .The copy [he] turned out is notably superior. . .*
>
> *We venture to congratulate the* Journal *on its special enterprise, and to express the hope that it indicates similar modification of methods and standards in other departments.* [27]

Hearst was more than pleased with the current state of his paper's "methods and standards." After the war, the *Journal* kept its grip on working-class readers with an editorial platform of pure Progressive politics. Hearst's paper championed such domestic issues as a graduated income tax, direct election of United States senators, and nationalization of mines, railroads, and telegraph lines coupled with "destruction of the criminal trusts." Foreign policies were based on the maintenance of a strong navy and the construction of an isthmian canal without European interference. All of these issues were popular with working-class men and women whom Hearst courted as regular readers. [28]

Hearst was no longer the callow Western newcomer. His papers were successful, his reputation for boldness recognized. The political views he had espoused in his papers led Democratic party leaders to view him as an ally. Now they sought his direct support as well. In the spring before the 1900 elections he conferred with party leaders who suggested quite pointedly that there was no successful Democratic paper in Chicago. Hearst was already contemplating Chicago

Left: Hearst snaps a photograph of a wrecked Spanish warship from a vessel off Santiago at the onset of the Spanish-American War.

Above: Hearst combined entertainment with hard news when reporting on the Spanish-American War.

THE WIZARD OF OOZE

Above: In reference to his involvement in muckraking, Harper's Weekly *depicts Hearst as "The Wizard of Ooze."*

Right: The cover of Puck *magazine caricatures Hearst as Buster Brown covering a goat with yellow paint.*

as the home of his third paper, but he believed that the paper must be started from scratch and must be on the stands in six weeks to be influential in the coming election.

In the opinion of one veteran journalist, "No one but W.R. Hearst with. . .his refusal to recognize the impossible, would have even considered starting a great metropolitan daily newspaper from scratch in six weeks at the turn of the century. Even in those days such a venture would ordinarily take months and possibly a year or more. Today it would be preceded by a couple of years of market surveys and months of advertising campaigns." [29]

Nevertheless, Hearst proceeded. First he sent his longtime business manager, Solomon Carvalho, and his most able editor, Arthur Brisbane, on to Chicago in advance. He gathered a group of reporters and editors to travel with him to Chicago, along with a cargo of new presses shipped from New York. Contracts were made for staff and supplies. He persuaded the Democratic presidential candidate, William Jennings Bryan, to push the button that started the presses for the first time. On July 4, 1900, the first edition of the Chicago *American* was distributed.

In late October, Hearst made his public debut as a political force, appearing at a rally in Madison Square Garden. Hearst made no speech, being responsible only for calling the throng to order and introducing the party chair. He appeared to enjoy his brief appearance in the political spotlight immensely, "laughing outright when some individual in the crowd yelled, 'Three cheers for Willie Hearst!'" [30]

No matter how enthusiastic the crowds, he held no hopes for Bryan's election. Undaunted by Bryan's loss in November, Hearst continued his close alliance with the leaders inside the Democratic party.

But his thoughts were not devoted exclusively to papers and politics. After 40 years of bachelorhood, William Randolph Hearst decided to marry. His bride, a New York City theatrical performer, was Millicent Veronica Willson.

Part Two Endnotes

1 Edwin Emery, *The Press in America* (Englewood Cliffs, N.J.: Prentice-Hall, 1962) 346.

2 Garth Jowett, *Film: The Democratic Art* (Boston: Little, Brown and Company, 1976) 16-17.

3 WRH to PAH, undated, PAH Papers, Bancroft.

4 WRH to GH, [1887], WRH Papers, Bancroft.

5 Swanberg, *Citizen Hearst*, 53.

6 Will Irwin, "The Fourth Current," *Collier's*, February 18, 1911, 14.

7 John Tebbel, *The Life and Good Times of William Randolph Hearst* (New York: E.P. Dutton, 1952) 99-100.

8 Swanberg, *Citizen Hearst*, 43.

9 Oscar Lewis, *The Big Four* (1938; New York: Knopf, 1946) 349.

10 Edmond D. Coblentz, *William Randolph Hearst: A Portrait in His Own Words* (New York: Simon & Schuster, 1952) 48.

11 WRH to GH, [1887], WRH Papers, Bancroft.

12 PAH to GH, August 7, 1888, PAH Papers, Bancroft.

13 Coblentz 34-35.

14 WRH to PAH, [1894], PAH Papers, Bancroft.

15 Tebbel 126.

16 W.A. Swanberg, *Pulitzer* (New York: Scribners, 1967) 205.

17 Irwin 18.

18 New York *Journal*, February 22, 1906.

19 Tebbel 116-117.

20 Swanberg, *Pulitzer*, 83.

21 New York *Journal*, November 8, 1896.

22 New York *Journal*, October 21, 1900.

23 Swanberg, *Pulitzer*, 224.

24 Marcus Wilkerson, *Public Opinion and the Spanish-American War: A Study in War Propaganda* (1932; New York: Russell & Russell, 1967) 33.

25 WRH to PAH, [1898], PAH Papers, Bancroft.

26 Emery 374.

27 *New York Times*, July 1, 1898.

28 Soon Jin Kim, "An Anatomy of the Hearst Press Campaign to Fortify an American Isthmian Canal," Diss., University of Maryland, 1982, 87.

29 George Murray, *The Madhouse on Madison Street* (Chicago: Follett Publishing Company, 1965) ix.

30 *New York Times*, October 28, 1900.

Part 3

THE HEARST EMPIRE

Phoebe Apperson Hearst was not pleased about her son's impending marriage. She had hoped that he would form an alliance with a woman from a prominent, wellborn family. Will had had one serious romance with a San Franciscan named Eleanor Calhoun during his years at Harvard. While Miss Calhoun's family was impeccable, descending from John C. Calhoun, statesman and former vice-president of the United States, her desire to pursue a stage career was completely unacceptable to Phoebe. George Hearst joined his wife in opposing the match and the relationship withered and eventually died.

Will's favorite recreation was attending the theater, where he met the attractive women his mother found so objectionable. Millicent Willson met Hearst in the autumn of 1896, when appearing with her sister, Anita, eight times a week at the Herald Square Theater in a musical called *The Girl from Paris*. Millicent later recalled that her mother opposed her first outing with Hearst because:

> *we were carefully supervised in those days and I recall [my mother] said, "Who is he? Some young fellow from out West somewhere, isn't he?" She insisted Anita come along or I couldn't go.*

> *Well, he took us down to the Journal—the New York Journal—we'd hardly heard of it, and he showed us over it, all over it. I hadn't the foggiest notion of what we were doing, walking miles on rough boards in thin, high-heeled evening slippers, and I thought my feet would kill me.*
>
> *Of course, this wasn't our idea of a good time. We wanted to go to Sherry's or Bustanoby's. More than that Anita kept whispering to me, "We're going to get thrown out of here, Milly, the way he behaves you'd think he owned it."*[1]

The Willson sisters discovered almost immediately that Hearst did indeed own the paper. Despite the pressure of his competition with Pulitzer, he continued to attend the theater almost nightly. Millicent and Anita, now assured of his status, often accompanied him to the *Journal* to witness the rearrangement of the next day's papers that Hearst found so irresistible.

Late in 1899, Hearst invited Millicent, Anita, and their parents on an extended holiday abroad. For Hearst, they were a fresh audience eager to share the sights of Europe. He never tired of overseas holidays, and preferred to bring a group of fellow travelers who could be depended upon to share his enthusiasm for

Above: Millicent Willson Hearst (1882-1974). Opposite: Hearst in hotel room while on the campaign trail.

cathedrals, art galleries, and other similar forms of Hearstian paradise.

Once Will and Millicent decided to marry, little planning was necessary, as the wedding was a small affair attended by approximately 30 guests. Orrin Peck served as Will's best man and Anita Willson was maid of honor for her 22-year-old sister. The service was held in Grace Episcopal Church in New York City on April 28, 1903, the day before Hearst's 40th birthday. Phoebe Hearst pleaded illness and remained in California, though she sent emeralds as a gift for the bride. Later in the day, the wedding couple embarked on a European honeymoon. In Paris they bought an automobile, still a rarity, and traveled through northern Italy.

A later stop in London brought Hearst's attention back to business. He had been pondering the wisdom of entering the national magazine market, which was booming the way newspapers had when he began his publishing career in the 1880s. The British magazine, *The Car,* inspired him to begin a similar automobiling magazine, which he christened *Motor.* The magazine was so successful it spawned a second Hearst publication, *Motor Boating.*

Other magazine titles were added to the Hearst stable, including *Cosmopolitan, Popular Mechanics, Harper's Bazaar* (purchased for the bargain price of $10,000), and *Good Housekeeping.* By the mid-1930s, nine Hearst magazines reached over 12.5 million American readers. An English division of the magazine company was created, which published *Connoisseur* and *Nash's* as well as British editions of *Good Housekeeping* and *Harper's Bazaar.*

When Will and Millicent returned from their wedding journey, they traveled to the Babicora ranch in Chihuahua and on to Mexico City, where they were received by the country's president, Porfirio Diaz. They traveled next to visit Phoebe Hearst at her hacienda outside Pleasanton, California and then returned to New York City to the four-story Lexington Avenue house Hearst had purchased in 1901.

Determined to prove herself a worthy wife and daughter-in-law, Millicent had given up her career upon her engagement. The official betrothal and wedding announcements omitted her theatrical background. Once wed, she dedicated her life to husband and children, genteel society and philanthropy, just as Phoebe had over 40 years earlier.

The Hearsts' first child, George Randolph, was born in New York City on April 10, 1904. The birth of her first grandson, who was named for her husband, softened Phoebe's character somewhat. Four more children, all boys, followed: William Randolph, Jr., in 1908, John Randolph in 1909, and twins, Randolph Apperson and David Whitmire in 1915.

Although the Hearsts lived in New York City and Phoebe had returned to California after closing her Washington residence, Will remained close to his mother and the family visited her Pleasanton estate frequently. Shortly after George's birth, Hearst proposed a visit to Phoebe, writing, "I want [the baby] to know his grandma. He knows the picture and kisses that, and it can't be very satisfactory just to lick the varnish off photographs. I think he would prefer the real article, and I think you would prefer the real baby."[2] As Hearst's business and political trips occupied more of his time, Millicent and the children began to stay at the Hacienda for extended periods, benefiting from the sunshine, country air and Phoebe Hearst's attention.

Left: Portrait of Millicent Veronica Willson. Above: Hearst and his bride, Millicent Willson, in 1903.

The Hearsts the night they hosted a costume party as a housewarming for their new flat on Riverside Drive.

On April 18, 1906, Millicent was staying at the Pleasanton ranch with her son, while Phoebe visited Paris and Will tended to business in New York City. When the night editor of the New York *American* (formerly the *Journal*) awakened Hearst at his Lexington Avenue apartment with the first news of the San Francisco earthquake, Hearst unaccountably dismissed its news value by explaining to the excited editor that tremors were commonplace in California. The *American* ran an editorial written by Hearst the next morning, which noted, "Californians don't wholly approve of earthquakes, but they prefer them to cyclones or tornadoes or floods or protracted heat or lightning storms. All of the earthquakes that have occurred in California since it was discovered. . .have not killed so many people as one or two great cyclones of the Middle West."[3]

Once Hearst realized the extent of the temblor's damage, he drew on all of the resources at his disposal. His Chicago, New York and Los Angeles newspapers sent well-publicized trains loaded with supplies from sympathetic subscribers. He sent telegraphic orders to Oakland directing the efforts to get the *Examiner* on the streets again. Hearst then left New York for Washington, where he submitted a bill (despite the fact that he represented a district in New York City) requesting federal funds for disaster relief and the construction of new government buildings in San Francisco. Upon reaching the devastated city, he saw the rubble that remained as the only sign of his hardwon *Examiner* building. No consolation was drawn from the fact that the *Chronicle* and *Call* were also burned out of their buildings.

Millicent wrote to Phoebe, reassuring her that the Hacienda escaped without much damage. Of the city, she wrote:

Little one story frame houses like in the mining camp are being put up and in these shacks are located some of the biggest firms of the city. . . .

Will is losing forty thousand dollars a month income from the Examiner *but thinks the paper will be making money again soon. Our [news]papers have done a great deal of good. They raised about a quarter of a million dollars for the sufferers and established relief camps and hospitals and supply stations and etc. Seventeen relief trains carrying food and clothing and doctors and nurses and hospital supplies and sewing machines and goods to be made up were sent by the papers into San Francisco. They were the first trains to arrive. . . .*

Our big hospital was taken over by the government, but we are still maintaining a maternity hospital. There are twenty-four women in it and five babies have been born. One is named Phoebe Hearst something and another was named Millicent Hearst something but there was no William Hearst as no boy babies have come along yet. . . .[4]

Once the crisis had passed, Hearst took his family on a trip to the San Simeon ranch. He derived great satisfaction from continuing the tradition of family visits to San Simeon, though Hearst's notion of camping had taken on more sybaritic overtones than his father had ever considered. On each of these family expeditions, the emphasis was on the benefits of fresh air, sunshine and salt water. But instead of using the blankets on the ground as George Hearst had favored, Will, Millicent, their family, and the domestic help retired in the evening to elaborate tents. Separate tents for dining, sleeping, and storage were pitched upon wooden flooring and partitioned into four rooms.

This tent village was grouped around "a great circus tent with board flooring covered with soft, warm rugs rich as those of a Bedouin chieftain's."[5] While at San Simeon, Hearst "amused himself by writing, directing and photographing cinema plays, using members of the family,

The Hearst Corporation acquired a number of magazines in addition to its numerous newspaper holdings.

Above: Millicent and twins, David Whitmire and Randolph Apperson.
Right: One of the glorious lupine fields in the countryside surrounding San Simeon.

guests, even. . .pets as actors, and showing pictures in the Big Top every night to the squealing glee of the youngsters." [6]

Setting up Hearst's camp was a laborious matter because he favored a site at the ranch that came to be known as Camp Hill, some five miles inland and nearly 1,600 feet above sea level. Millicent wrote enthusiastically to Phoebe of the visit they made to San Simeon after the earthquake:

> *We are now stopping over night at San Rafael on our way up the coast. We have been down the coast as far as Paso Robles and from there to the ranch where we had a very delightful time. I don't think any place in California has suited the baby as well as the ranch. He played on the beach every day and got sunburned and as strong and healthy as a little indian. We also enjoyed ourselves. We camped out on the Burnett [peak] and on the hill tops. We were there two weeks and enjoyed every moment of the time. . . .*
>
> *We hate to leave California. . . .We dread going back to the hot red brick houses and the dusty streets of New York. . . .[7]*

However reluctant the Hearst family was to return to the East Coast, it was necessary because of William Randolph Hearst's growing political interests. His appearance at the Democratic presidential convention in 1900 had whetted Hearst's appetite for political office, an ambition he had harbored since college days. His loyalty to the William Jennings Bryan candidacy won him a seat in the House of Representatives during the 1902 elections. Hearst won re-election two years later from the same West Side district of New York City.

Hearst had always prided himself on his individualism and his influence, but this philosophy did not work to his advantage as a freshman Congressional representative. His strong and straightforward endorsement of liberal Progressive issues, from public ownership of utilities to the eight-hour workday, brought a wary response from most of his Democratic colleagues.

Above: Hearst newspaper ad.
Right: Crowd shows support of Hearst for governor in 1906.
Far right: Hearst campaigning for governor of New York.

He secured an appointment to the House Labor Committee through his labor connections, which further alienated his colleagues who were dependent upon the traditional method of working through the House party leader, John Sharp Williams. Hearst's most effective work in the House was accomplished on this committee through his organization of a "small group of radical Democrats, who did his floor work and followed his lead on committees. In Hearst's own committee appearances, he surprised reporters with his presentation and command of the issues."[8]

Before he took his seat for a second term in Congress, Hearst made a concerted bid for the office of Mayor of New York City. Hearst had developed into an amazingly effective stump speaker, wooing the working-class vote from the podium as well as the editorial pages. The non-Hearst New York papers did not endorse him; the *Times* viewed the successful tide of his candidacy with alarm. In one of several attempts to discredit him, the *Times* noted his large support among East Side working class neighborhoods, where Hearst's carriage was stopped one day by this chant from his supporters:

> *Hoist, Hoist,*
> *He is not the woist;*
> *We are for Hoist,*
> *Last and foist.*[9]

The consensus among contemporary observers and political historians is that Hearst actually won this closely contested race against incumbent George McClellan, but Tammany, the political machine that controlled New York, committed several kinds of vote fraud to return their incumbent to office. The final count revealed that Hearst had lost by only 3,000 votes out of a total of 600,000 cast.

Hearst returned to Congress, but he had lost what little interest he displayed in the legislative process. His appearances on the floor and in committee were few; his small coalition of radical Progressives had unraveled. Hearst was now determined to run for President.

He owned the strongest Democratic papers in San Francisco, New York, Chicago, Los Angeles, and Boston, whose combined circulation reached two million readers per day. The Baltimore *Sun,* a paper not owned by Hearst, ran an editorial naming Hearst, William Jennings Bryan and Theodore Roosevelt as the country's three major politicians.[10]

The most direct route to the White House appeared to be through the governorship of New York. Hearst won the Democratic party nomination in 1906, greatly upsetting conservatives in the party. In a remarkable turnabout, Hearst now courted the crooked Tammany machine. Although his campaign reiterated

The Hearst family demonstrating patriotic fervor during World War I.

Hearst's endorsement of labor unions, public ownership of utilities, and trust-busting, his support from radical Progressives virtually disappeared after he approached Tammany. Resentful of his journalistic power and suspicious of his independent methods, the Democratic party leaders in New York opposed his candidacy.

Hearst once again lost by the amazingly close margin of 60,000 votes out of 1.5 million cast, effectively ending his Presidential chances. As an independent, Hearst tried again in 1908 and 1912 to win the presidency, but his efforts were doomed. His public political career consisted of his two terms in the House, but his private political career continued until his death. He remained a powerful figure, courted by Democratic candidates not only for public endorsements in his newspapers, but also for his private affirmations to party leaders behind the scenes.

Hearst's pace was so hectic that Millicent became concerned and wrote to Phoebe in 1907:

> . . .We have been having a very lively time here. There has been a campaign on and a [financial] panic and Will has been in both. One night Will was trying to learn his speech in time to go to six meetings while. . .Edward Clark [Hearst's financial manager] was explaining how everything was going to pieces in Wall Street and we would all be broke in the morning. . . .Will thinks the situation has cleared somewhat but he never leaves the telephone until after banking hours. . . .
>
> We have been neglecting our flat on account of our other troubles but your nice letter and the offer of the tapestries got us interested in the flat again and we went up there today to see where we could put such lovely things. . . .[11]

The "flat" Millicent mentioned in this letter actually consisted of the top three floors of the posh Clarendon apartment building at 137 Riverside Drive. Hearst's habitual acquisition of antiquities and works of art, as well as the birth of their second child, made the move from Lexington Avenue imperative. The newest of the Hearst residences was enormous, encompassing over 33,000 square feet, and soon was filled with Hearst's latest purchases from the auction houses in New York and Europe.

Although Hearst no longer made news as a politician, he continued to impress friends and enemies alike with the power and scope of his journalistic empire. As his energies were once again concentrated on the production and distribution of news, he considered the potential of motion pictures as a means of reporting the news.

American newsreels produced by William Randolph Hearst flourished from 1914 through the mid-1950s and continued to be shown in theaters until 1967. The producers of "actualities," as the first newsreels were called, found that major news events could be enhanced or even recreated in studios using special effects. As motion picture technology advanced, it became possible to capture news events as they occurred.

Although Edgar Hatrick, the Hearst executive in charge of photographic services, had counseled Hearst to begin a newsreel as early as 1911, the first news event filmed for a Hearst company was Woodrow Wilson's inauguration early in 1913. Hearst then joined forces with Colonel William Selig, who had first combined journalism with motion pictures in 1903. Advertising for the February 28, 1914, premiere promised:

> *Every week in the year. . .the big events of the whole world will be caught in the happening by Selig moving picture cameras, operated by the trained news gatherers of Hearst's great International News Service which covers the entire globe. . . .These news pictures, throbbing with live news interest in every foot of film, will be released to you weekly.*[12]

Although successful, the Hearst-Selig partnership was short-lived. By January, 1916, Hearst had combined forces with Vitagraph, producing *The Hearst-Vitagraph Weekly Series*. By mid-1916, this venture folded and Hearst released his own films for the remainder of the year under the title *The International Weekly*.

At the beginning of 1917, Hearst joined forces with a former rival, Pathé, but this alliance only lasted one year. From 1918 until 1920, Hearst remained independent, producing *The International Newsreel*. The Hearst name was conspicuously absent from this latest venture, leading his rivals to speculate that Hearst's opposition to American intervention in World War I had cost him viewers.[13]

By 1918 four newsreel companies had survived the fluctuations of the early years: Hearst, Pathé, Universal and Fox. These four, joined by Paramount's 1927 entry, would greatly influence the perception of major events by American viewers in the next three decades.[14]

Hearst and Louis B. Mayer were friends as well as successful business partners.

Top: Newsreel operator at Metrotone News, Fox Studio, New York City, 1938.

Above: This ad announced Hearst's first venture into filmed news as well as the first known use of the word newsreel.

Virtually from its inception, the newsreel followed the format and the style of current newspapers. It emphasized the most sensational events for lead stories, using large, easily understood headlines, and providing specialized features on homemaking and sporting events. Early newsreel companies, duplicating the management structure of newspapers, employed print journalists, editors, and camera operators. Hearst's journalistic style had a major impact on the format newsreels used because he was the only major newspaper publisher who entered the field.[15]

Between 1927 and 1929, Hearst produced separate newsreels for two studios, Universal and Metro-Goldwyn-Mayer. In 1929, as part of the Cosmopolitan Films contract he made with MGM, Hearst agreed to produce two newsreels exclusively for that studio. The first production, a silent, was entitled *The MGM International Newsreel*. It was targeted for smaller, rural theaters that had not yet installed sound equipment. The second newsreel was a sound production entitled *Hearst Metrotone News*, which became the standard at MGM's growing number of theaters.

In 1915, Hearst's uncanny timing, perhaps inherited from his prospector father, led him to the production of movies. His financial risk was relatively low, as his first ventures in the nascent picture industry were linked to his successful chain of newspapers. In 1913 the Chicago *Tribune,* feeling pressured by Hearst's *American,* published a newspaper serial story called *The Adventures of Kathlyn.* The twist came when the *Tribune* announced that its readers could also see the serial, which had been filmed in biweekly episodes by the Chicago-based Selig Polyscope Company. The *Tribune* reported a remarkable 10 percent increase in circulation, which sent competitors scrambling for their own newspaper/film combinations.

Hearst, in his inimitable style, immediately adopted the idea and expanded upon it. He contracted with the Pathé Film Company to produce *The Perils of Pauline,* which is remembered today as the classic of the early silent motion picture serials. An advertising campaign promoted the parallel venture widely, calling *Pauline* the "novel you can see in stirring MOTION PICTURES." Hearst is said to have contributed to the development of *Pauline's* plot. He also attended the March, 1914, premiere in New York City. The serial was an instant success in theaters, proving the trade advertising slogan, "Pauline Pulls People."[16]

If Hearst needed additional evidence of the serial's popularity, it was demonstrated the day Pearl White, the actress who played Pauline, was unintentionally set adrift in a balloon. A strong wind and a loosely tied rope sent the actress aloft over New York City during the filming of a scene. Showing as much pluck as Pauline in dangerous circumstances, White controlled her descent to a vacant lot by letting gas out of the balloon. An overly enthusiastic crowd had gathered in the lot and surged toward White as she landed. "One man snatched my purse for a souvenir. . . . Another man told him to return it and hit him when he refused. The friends of the first man came to his help and about ten fights ensued. Another man took out his penknife and cut a big

Above: A group of MGM starlets posed on a sound truck to promote Hearst's Metrotone sound production newsreel.

Left: Exterior of Hearst's Astoria Studio in New York.

In an advertisement in a trade publication, Hearst announces his intention to "make movies."

piece of my coat; this, also, for a souvenir. Others saw him and did the same thing. . . .If it hadn't been for the mounted police coming to my rescue, that would have been my last peril. . . ."[17]

While the *Kathlyn* serial had boosted circulation for the *Tribune*, *The Perils of Pauline* did not do the same for the Hearst papers. One early cinema historian proposed the theory that "the conservative *Tribune* used the motion picture to reach into the emotion-hungry nickelodeon audiences. The vivid Hearst newspapers, Brisbaned and comic-stripped, already had that class of following and the motion picture could add nothing to their pulling power."[18]

The success of the film version was more than enough for Hearst. His company and Pathé began work immediately on a follow-up series designed to capitalize on *Pauline's* momentum. *The Exploits of Elaine*, a 1915 production again featuring Pearl White, was also short on plot but compensated with an abundance of action.

Another Hearst-Pathé production in 1916 was *Beatrice Fairfax*, starring Grace Darling. The name of this newest serial heroine was chosen for its recognition value. For the past 15 years, Hearst had run an advice-to-the-lovelorn column in his papers. The advice was dispensed by a Hearst staff member, Marie Manning, who used Beatrice Fairfax as her pen name. The column proved so popular that it was advertised with this jingle:

> *Just write to Beatrice Fairfax*
> *Whenever you're in doubt;*
> *Just write to Beatrice Fairfax*
> *And she will help you out.*[19]

The serial version of *Beatrice Fairfax* ran in a "photostrip" in the daily papers. Frames from the film were reproduced along with the narrative, which further popularized the serial as visual entertainment.

The last of the monumental Hearst-Pathé serial films was the 1917 production of *Patria,* starring Irene Castle. The dancing partner of Vernon Castle, Irene was billed as "the best known woman in America today." The phenomenal success of the husband-and-wife dancing team led to the popularity of ballroom dancing and the proliferation of clothing, candy, cosmetics, nightclubs, hairstyles, shoes, tooth powder, and other goods and services endorsed by one or both Castles. While her husband served with the Royal Air Force during World War I, Irene Castle signed a contract with Hearst-Pathé and began filming at the Fort Lee, New Jersey, studios. She described the plot of *Patria* as:

> *A little jewel. I was Patria Channing, the sole heir to one hundred million dollars I didn't know about and the sole survivor of the 'Fighting Channings,' a family of munitions-makers dedicated to American Freedom. Warner Oland [later to play Charlie Chan] played the grimacing Baron Huroki, who schemed to have me replaced by a villainess named Elaine (who by coincidence was my exact double) who would put my little bundle of a hundred million dollars at the disposal of him and his Mexican confederates.*[20]

Hearst footed the $90,000 bill for the production of *Patria,* which had 15 chapters. In the course of the serial, Patria finally rescued the United States almost single-handedly, but the film was meant as a warning to American citizens to exercise vigilance against these two countries. Hearst's unfavorable opinion of Mexico was probably formed during the period immediately before *Patria* was filmed. Pancho Villa and his compatriots were responsible for a number of depredations at Hearst's huge Mexican ranches.

The film was banned in some parts of the country because it was considered too extreme. President Woodrow Wilson asked Hearst to withdraw the film and edit out the virulent anti-Japanese scenes. Hearst complied, but the film never met his expectations for its success. The editing affected the film's momentum and created confusion. "The result [was] that the film appeared primarily anti-Mexican—even to an Oriental-appearing advance guard with Japanese uniforms and Mexican names. To be anti-Mexican was not distressing to [Wilson] administration officials at the time. . . .In fact, [American soldiers] under Pershing were in Mexico when the picture was released."[21]

Top: Greta Garbo in her first American film, The Torrent, *made in 1926.*

Above: Advertisement for the film, a Hearst Cosmopolitan production.

The Hearst Empire

Cities with the earliest Hearst papers were San Francisco (1887), New York (1895), Chicago (1900), Los Angeles and Boston (both 1904). In 1902 he changed the name of the New York *Journal* to the *American*. Ten years later he entered the South with the purchase of the Atlanta *Daily Georgian*. In 1913 he acquired the San Francisco *Call*. The Washington *Times* and Boston Daily *Advertiser* were added in 1917.

In 1922 the Hearst Corporation marked the greatest year of its growth by acquiring five papers: the Rochester *Journal*, Oakland Post-*Enquirer*, Los Angeles *Herald*, Washington *Herald* and Syracuse *Journal* and beginning a sixth, the tabloid (in philosophy and format) New York *Mirror*.

Two years later Hearst bought the Albany *Times-Union*, San Antonio *Light*, and Milwaukee *Sentinel*. In 1927 he bought a Pittsburgh paper and the following year acquired the Omaha *Bee-News*.

In 1937, 50 years after he began his career in San Francisco, Hearst publishing ventures reached their apex. Twenty-five daily papers with a combined circulation of over five million readers, and 17 Sunday papers with nearly six million readers bore the Hearst name.

In addition to the direct ownership of newspapers, the Hearst Corporation also operated wire services, syndicates, feature services, paper mills, and distribution centers. Hearst also owned and distributed the *American Weekly*, a Sunday supplement, to non-Hearst papers. At its height, the *American Weekly* reached 30 million homes each Sunday.

As of October, 1986, the Hearst Corporation holds 135 businesses including magazines, broadcasting, newspapers, books, business publishing and cable communications.

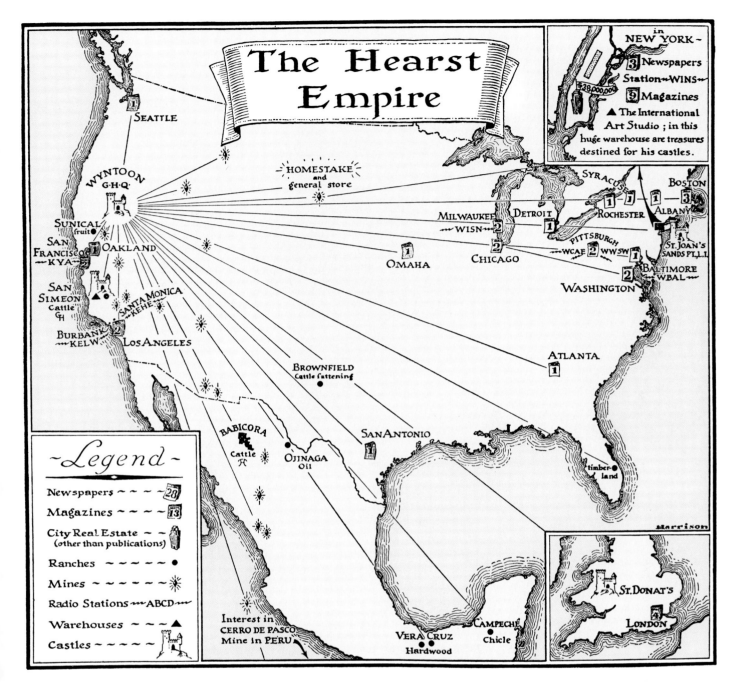

This map, which appeared in the October 1935, issue of Fortune *magazine, shows how Hearst-owned businesses and properties radiate from Wyntoon in northern California to every corner of the U.S. and Mexico, even spanning the Atlantic to London.*

In a scene from Cain & Mabel, *1936, Marion Davies prepares to slap Clark Gable while cocktail party guests look on.*

If Hearst had given his filmmaking the same enormous energy and obsessive preoccupation he gave his newspapers, his movies might have been successful enough to accord him a place in film history at least on a level with [noted British producer] Alexander Korda, a man who had similar tastes in subject matter. . . .

[Hearst] was one of the first to use technicolor, to do a musical, to insist upon historical accuracy (even though it was not an ethic of his newspaper publishing), but he is seldom cited in film histories for any of this. . . .[22]

Hearst's first Cosmopolitan motion picture studio was located in a mammoth brick building that covered an entire city block in New York City between Second Avenue and 125th Street. A popular German *beirgarten* called Sulzer's Harlem River Park Casino had once flourished on the site. When Prohibition caused the business to close, Hearst renovated the property, filling it with expensive cameras and other film-making equipment.[23]

In December of 1917, he attended a special screening of *Runaway, Romany,* a film produced by friend and fellow newspaper publisher, Paul Block, that starred Marion Davies. Hearst had met Davies nearly two years earlier, and in the ensuing period became deeply attached to her. Block was pessimistic about the potential of *Runaway,* which was the first venture in filmmaking for both him and Davies. Hearst, however, saw a wealth of possibilities that could be improved upon in the next Davies film. At the end of the screening, Hearst realized two things: he wanted to produce Davies's next picture and he was more taken with her than ever.

From that moment, Hearst became virtually obsessed with the idea of making Davies a star of the first magnitude. Every resource he possessed would be employed. His wealth bought properties to film and experienced screenwriters, his theater and film connections provided experienced actors and technicians, his art objects graced her sets, his newspapers publicized her name, and he entertained their peers in the film industry at his various estates.

Pathe continued to produce serials both independently and with Hearst's support, but by 1917 Hearst decided to branch out on his own to begin production of feature-length motion pictures. His company was initially named International Films, but near the end of the decade Hearst changed the name to Cosmopolitan Pictures.

Hearst moved into the picture business the same way he had conquered publishing: he offered high salaries to attract talented workers and supplied them with ample operating budgets. The first actress he signed was Alma Rubens, a 20-year-old native of San Francisco whose true name was Alma Smith. Famed for her classical beauty, Rubens had appeared in D.W. Griffith's 1916 epic, *Intolerance.*

One film historian who assessed Hearst's career in this field decided:

Top: *Huntley Gordon watches Joan Crawford frolic with her boy friends in a scene from* Our Dancing Daughters, *a 1928 film by MGM, formerly entitled* The Dancing Girl.

Left: *Advertisement for Hearst's biggest box-office success,* Manhattan Melodrama.

Bottom: *Marion Davies and Leslie Howard in a scene from MGM's 1931 movie,* Five and Ten.

Marion Davies, whose true name was Marion Cecilia Douras, was born in Brooklyn on January 3, 1897. A stunning beauty with blonde hair and blue eyes, she made her Broadway debut in 1911 in Charles Dillingham's production of *The Lady and the Slipper*. By 1915 she was appearing in another Dillingham production entitled *Chin-Chin*. In mid-June she opened in the 1916 edition of Florenz Ziegfeld's *Follies*, where it is generally believed Hearst first saw her. She was able to parlay her *Follies* experience into a role in the Irving Berlin revue, *Stop! Look! Listen!*. Fred Lawrence Guiles describes Davies during this period as a member of:

> the vanguard of a new kind of young woman, soon to be emancipated from more than her bustle. She radiated vitality and wholesome good cheer along with a latent (later realized) flair for parody and comedy that would keep her working for the next twenty-two years. . . .To nearly everyone who met her, she seemed as effervescent as champagne and it would seem completely in key with her personality when she developed such a taste for that beverage.[24]

Top: A Davies Photoplay *cover from 1933.*
Middle & left: Lobby card and trade ad promoting Marion Davies.
Above: Davies in Ziegfeld's Follies.

Portrait of Marion Davies by Sarony.

Cover of one of the editions of the Marion Davies film books.

Davies was working overtime. The filming of *Runaway* was sandwiched in between her stage appearances during the summer of 1916. While Hearst prepared to launch her career in earnest with a suitable property, Davies returned to the Broadway stage for three successive 1917 productions: *Oh, Boy, Miss 1917,* and *Words and Music.* The premiere of her first Cosmopolitan production, *Cecilia of the Pink Roses,* was made at the Rivoli Theater on June 3, 1918, with a Hearstian gesture: the picture screen was surrounded with thousands of pink roses whose fragrance was blown toward the audience by discreetly placed fans. Hearst devised an unprecedented plan to book the film into 12 different theaters in New York City at once.

Hearst's New York *American* declared the film a "masterpiece" and noted ". . .there were few dry eyes at the Rivoli Theater yesterday when the vision of Marion Davies faded on the screen." The *New York Times* somewhat laconically stated: "There is no objection to Miss Davies. She is by no means a sensational screen actress, but she fills the requirements of her part. . . ."

One of Davies's first interviews was published in the October, 1919, issue of *Photoplay.* The article described a visit to Davies, in her posh new home on Riverside Drive, in the breathless style such magazines adopted. The article neglected to mention that Hearst had purchased the house as a permanent residence for Davies and her mother and sisters. After exclaiming over her dazzling good looks, the interviewer discovered Davies's stammer:

Part Three Endnotes

1 Adela Rogers St. Johns, *The Honeycomb* (Garden City: Doubleday, 1969) 131-2.

2 Coblentz 68-69.

3 New York *American* quoted in Gordon Thomas and Max Morgan Witts, *The San Francisco Earthquake* (New York: Stein and Day, 1971) 83.

4 Millicent Hearst (MH) to PAH, [April, 1906], HF Papers, Bancroft.

5 John K. Winkler, *William Randolph Hearst: A New Appraisal* (New York: Hastings House, 1955) 183.

6 Winkler 183.

7 MH to PAH, July 30, 1906, HF Papers, Bancroft.

8 David Sarasohn, "Power Without Glory: Hearst in the Progressive Era," *Journalism Quarterly,* 53.3 (1976) 477.

9 Swanberg, *Citizen Hearst,* 236.

10 Sarasohn 474. Historian Arthur Schlesinger, Jr., has described Hearst's political beliefs as "follow[ing] a long trajectory from left to right," but recent revisionist thinking postulates that Hearst's political views actually changed very little from the turn of the century until his death fifty years later. Arthur Schlesinger, Jr., *The Age of Roosevelt* vol. III (Boston: Houghton-Mifflin, 1960) 84.

11 MH to PAH, October 29, 1907, HF Papers, Bancroft.

12 *Moving Picture World,* March 7, 1914, quoted in Raymond Fielding, *The American Newsreel: 1911-1967* (Norman: University of Oklahoma Press, 1972) 86.

13 *Time,* November 23, 1936, 25.

14 The names of newsreels produced by these companies were *Fox-Movietone News, Hearst Metrotone News,* (later retitled *News of the Day), Paramount News* ("The Eyes and Ears of the World"), *Pathé News* and *Universal News.*

15 Fielding 135. Also, according to Fielding, "The use of the word "newsreel" in the [ads for the *International Newsreel*] was probably the first occasion in which this term was used as part of a commercial trade name, although we do see it used in the descriptive term in a *Hearst-Selig News Pictorial* advertisement as early as March 7, 1914. (Many years later the Hearst organization claimed to have used the term as part of its trademark as early as 1914.)"

16 Kalton Lahue, *Continued Next Week: A History of the Moving Picture Serial* (Norman: University of Oklahoma Press, 1964) 8.

17 Lahue 12.

18 Terry Ramsaye, *A Million and One Nights: A Modern Classic* (1926; New York: Simon & Schuster 1986) 662.

19 Ishbel Ross, *Ladies of the Press* (1936; New York: Arno Press, 1974) 79. Another 1916 Hearst-Pathé venture, *The Mysteries of Myra,* began the trend toward passive heroines. Myra was dependent upon the actions of others for her salvation, primarily her quick-thinking fiancé who always intervened in the nick of time.

20 Irene Castle, *Castles in the Air* (1958; New York: Da Capo Press, 1980) 145.

21 Raymond William Stedman, *The Serials: Suspense and Drama by Installment* (Norman: University of Oklahoma Press, 1971) 41.

22 Fred Lawrence Guiles, *Marion Davies* (New York: McGraw-Hill, 1972) 120.

23 Winkler 227.

24 Guiles 43-44.

25 Delight Evans, "Galatea on Riverside Drive," *Photoplay,* October, 1919, 36.

To know that she stuttered. . .made her a little less Olympian — the goddess actually moved, talked, laughed and everything.

This lovely lisper was Marion Davies, whom all our photographers like to picture as a sort of Queen Louise of the lenses — always with an expression of supreme hauteur, with one white hand raised a la Milo — a symphony of sovereign femininity. The place, her home on Riverside Drive. . .a white palace in the 300 block.

I suspect that her great joy in this home of hers is in manipulating the little lift that carries you from height to superheight — from the salon with the marble fountain on the first to a hall of mirrors, on the second and to a library on the third floor — and I liked her best in the library. It's a long room in old blue — lined with books. Hundreds of books — tiers of them on four walls. Books in rare bindings, first editions, books of history, travel, satire and fiction.

"I-I'll read all of these when I'm an old wo-woman," she said and reached up and took down a book.[25]

With Davies's career successfully underway, Hearst realized that Cosmopolitan Pictures would need to form new alliances in the rapidly growing film industry. In mid-1919, Hearst struck a deal with Adolf Zukor's Artcraft and Paramount Pictures Corporation to distribute all of Cosmopolitan's productions. The alliance between Hearst and Paramount assured a regular venue for Cosmopolitan productions.

In the midst of his first ventures into feature-length motion picture production, Hearst was called to his mother's deathbed. Ill with influenza since a Christmas visit to her son and his family in New York, Phoebe Hearst was stricken during the world-wide epidemic that claimed more than half a million lives in the United States alone. On April 13, 1919, Phoebe Apperson Hearst died at her Pleasanton estate in California at the age of 76. Her only child was the principal heir to her estate, including 11 million dollars and the title to the vast San Simeon ranch.

Hearst with his firstborn, George Randolph, at the Hacienda.

THE GOLDEN YEARS

William Randolph Hearst's fondness for imposing, yet comfortable, residences dated to his college years, when he made enthusiastic plans with his mother for the Hacienda del Pozo de Verona and their Washington house. Of all the property Hearst now inherited, San Simeon was by far his favorite. Early in 1919 he declared himself "tired of. . .camping in tents" at the coastal property and consulted Julia Morgan, a San Francisco architect of some renown, about building on the site.

Much has been made of the contrast between Hearst's initial request for a single "bungalow" and the formidable estate that grew in its place. But the idea of a single structure, however grand, was abandoned very quickly in favor of a more ambitious plan. Three guesthouses and a central structure, Casa Grande, were built and linked, as Hearst requested, by a "plan of walks and flower beds or landscape features. . .that will bring all of the structures together into a harmonious whole."

Millicent Hearst suggested that the formal name of the estate be *Las Estrellas*, but it was discovered that the name was already in use at a neighboring ranch. In its place Hearst chose the name *La Cuesta Encantada*,

Spanish for The Enchanted Hill, although he usually referred to his hilltop estate as simply "the ranch." [1]

More than 20 years of intense collaboration between Morgan and her client would produce constantly shifting plans for a main house, guesthouses, indoor and outdoor swimming pools, shelters for a growing menagerie, barracks for the construction workers, warehouses, reservoir, a small village with houses for permanent staff, and a mile-long pergola. In addition to the estate that exists today, Hearst and Morgan had plans for guesthouses and wings for Casa Grande that were never built.

Julia Morgan accepted the San Simeon commission at the midpoint of a varied and prolific career. By 1919 she had been practicing nearly 20 years and had at least 350 other private residences, institutions, churches, estates, and community buildings to her credit. Nine years younger than Hearst, Morgan was raised in Oakland, California. She studied civil engineering at the University of California at Berkeley, where she was obliged to be chaperoned by her brother while attending classes. She graduated in 1894 as the first woman to earn a Berkeley degree in the discipline.

Left: Hearst and his visitors frequently swam in the heated water of the Neptune Pool.

Above: Hearst and his dog, Helena, seated on the edge of a fountain at Wyntoon.

*Above: Hearst with Julia Morgan, the architect
who designed his San Simeon estate.*
Right: Tile design drawn by Morgan.

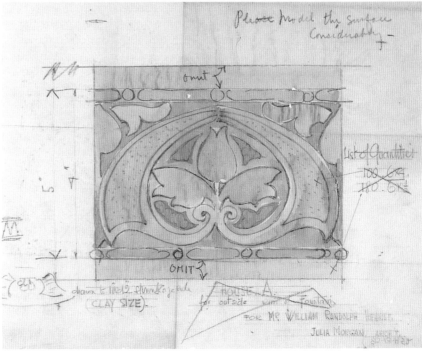

Upon the advice of one of her instructors, architect Bernard Maybeck, Morgan traveled to Paris to study at the *École Nationale et Spéciale des Beaux-Arts*. When she arrived in 1896, she was refused admission because *Beaux-Arts* administrators had never conceived of allowing women to study at the institution. Morgan was eventually admitted in November of 1898 and advanced to the top class within a year. During a stay in Paris in 1899, Phoebe Hearst visited the homesick and discouraged young woman, whom she knew from Berkeley, and offered to be her financial sponsor. Although Morgan declined the offer, Hearst's gesture encouraged her to persevere. In 1902 she became the first woman to receive *École des Beaux-Arts* certification in architecture.

When she returned to San Francisco, Julia Morgan joined the staff of architect John Galen Howard. He had opened an office in Berkeley after winning (by default) the Phoebe Apperson Hearst Architectural Competition to design a master building plan for the University of California. Morgan drew the elevations and designed the decorative details for the Mining Building, commissioned by Phoebe Hearst in memory of her mining magnate husband. The Greek Theater on the Berkeley campus, also a Hearst gift, was the young architect's next design under Howard's aegis.

In 1904 Morgan opened her own practice in San Francisco. As her career developed, she began work on a number of residential commissions in the Piedmont, Claremont, and Berkeley neighborhoods. Morgan was also commissioned by Phoebe Hearst to finish the Pleasanton Hacienda and to begin work on one of Phoebe's last philanthropic gestures, the YWCA (Young Women's Christian Association) conference center at Pacific Grove, called Asilomar.

Top: Sketches for the bell towers on the Castle's main building, Casa Grande.
Right: Tile used for stair risers in Casa del Sol.

Julia Morgan's rigorous training in classical architecture at the *École des Beaux-Arts,* as well as her considerable experience working with reinforced concrete, made her the obvious choice for the work Hearst envisioned at San Simeon. Her reputation for respecting the wishes of her clients and her diplomatic personality further ensured her success with Hearst. Morgan continued to practice architecture full time from her San Francisco office, devoting her weekends to the on-site supervision at San Simeon.

As the project grew, Morgan found herself increasingly involved in the operation of the estate as well as its design. Funds from Hearst flowed through her office for the purchase of everything from Spanish antiquities and Hoover vacuum cleaners to Icelandic moss to feed the reindeer in the hilltop zoo. She hired not only the construction and warehouse workers, but the household staff as well.

Hearst lived in "A" House, the first of the guesthouses to be constructed, until Casa Grande was ready for occupancy. Severe rainstorms lashed the hilltop during February of 1927, revealing inadequacies in the heating system. After the first storm, Hearst dictated a letter to Morgan, suggesting that the doors to "A" House be made "water and draft proof with metal weather strips. If antique iron doors [do] not permit this, don't use antique iron. Let's have COMFORT AND HEALTH before so much art. The art won't do us any good if we are all dead of pneumonia."[2]

The massive construction site inspired this already avid collector to new heights. The flood of his purchases from Europe became so great that Morgan and her staff members designed an inventory system to work in concert with the International Studio Art Corporation, a subsidiary of the Hearst Corporation. This operation had a warehouse and offices in New York, where staff members

arranged for newly arrived European shipments to be transported either by rail across the country or by ship to ports at San Pedro or San Francisco and then to San Simeon.

Morgan had reinforced the wharf built by George Hearst in 1878, adding a railroad siding so that shipments could be unloaded smoothly and rolled to the series of warehouses she had designed and constructed. Here her staff members photographed and inventoried new shipments, then placed them in storage. Eventually some of these architectural elements and art objects were indeed installed in San Simeon or other Hearst estates. Some were sent to Hollywood for use on movie sets or to other cities for loan to museums. Still other shipments were never uncrated. By 1930, the warehouses at San Simeon were full.

A small village of Spanish-style houses, designed by Julia Morgan, grew up near the warehouses for the families of Hearst's long-term employees. Domestic workers were eventually housed in an entire wing of Casa Grande. Hearst suggested that Morgan make these rooms large enough "to relieve the discomforts which our best help now experience and which make it difficult to keep them on the Hill."[3]

Left: Hearst in Europe on an antique-collecting trip in 1934.

Bottom: Hearst purchased this ornately carved bed on a buying trip in 1920.

Right: The Castle's indoor Roman Pool.

Hearst, on the Road to the San Simeon

Above: Hearst spent many hours riding through the ranch lands he so dearly loved.

Right: The impressive façade of Casa Grande, *the main building at San Simeon.*

Initially the construction laborers lived in tents, which were later replaced with crude barracks. Morgan had the responsibility not only for hiring construction workers, but also for keeping them occupied during their Sundays off. Hearst forbade the workers to "wander over the ranch or to fish or to hunt. . . .They shall confine themselves to their legitimate business on the property."[4] With her options severely limited, Morgan hit upon the idea of showing movies in the remote location. "I have tried a moving picture show once a week. . . which has been well worth the money in keeping down 'turn-over'. The operator brings his own machine, pays his expenses and shows seven reels for $30.00."[5]

Hearst was never fond of living in the East, and so found little reason to continue to reside in New York with his political dreams in ashes and his marriage cooling. Millicent Hearst divided her time between the Riverside Drive apartment in New York and the former O.H.P. Belmont estate at Sands Point, Long Island. She traveled only infrequently to California. A great deal of her time was taken up with the Milk Fund, a charitable organization she had founded. For several reasons, Hearst found it simpler to return to San Simeon for increasingly longer periods of time. His inclination to travel, whether for business or pleasure, coupled with lavish use of telegrams, kept him apprised of his far-flung ventures and his family.

The Construction of Casa Grande

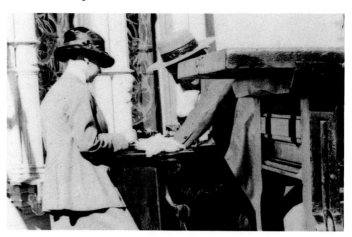

Julia Morgan's office records reveal a variety of at least 30 separate commissions from the Hearst family, from radio stations and newspaper buildings to ranch houses and Beverly Hills swimming pools. The most famous of these commissions was, of course, San Simeon. Hearst and Morgan conferred on site (top right) and by extensive use of letters and telegrams.

This late-1920s aerial view of the hilltop at the far right illustrates the scope of Hearst's San Simeon home, including the barracks for laborers in the foreground.

In the area where the Roman Pool is now situated, Morgan originally designed a garden, which was replaced by plans for an outdoor pool. The first pool constructed proved too small for Hearst's taste and was supplanted by the larger Roman Pool (middle right), which is shown here just after the Janus concrete lamp standards were installed in 1939.

Construction of a coastal highway between Cambria and Carmel began in 1922 and was not completed until 1937. The bridge spanning San Simeon creek (below) is shown here during its construction.

Top & above: Hearst takes a break from a croquet game at Wyntoon to look over and make notes on the daily log (left) that his personal secretary, Joseph Willicombe, kept of each day's important business.

Hearst purchased the former O.H.P. Belmont estate at Sands Point, Long Island.

One of his newspaper executives, Harry M. Bitner, recalled the usual method by which he conducted business with Hearst:

From six to a dozen times a year I visited Mr. Hearst for several days at a time, usually in California. I used to take with me briefcases filled with files on many subjects. Mr. Hearst was never in a hurry to talk after I arrived. He wanted me to rest for a day or two, perhaps to gain a better perspective. Then, during a full afternoon or evening, we would sit down and I would try to summarize, from the files I had brought, each problem or question. When each of my little speeches was ended, he gave his answer, succinct but comprehensive. If I did not always agree, he would listen courteously, analyze my comments, then usually reaffirm his previous decision. . .

He never said, 'Let's talk it over,' or 'Take it up later.' He always gave me a definite answer.[6]

If any of the army of Hearst employees doubted Hearst's control over the editorial policy of his vast number of papers, they soon found that he was in the habit of firing off letters of praise or blame directly to the employee in question. With his quick mind and capacity for detail, Hearst kept abreast of his many publications, assisted by secretary Joseph Willicombe. Even though the number of newspapers in his chain had risen dramatically, Hearst had scarcely altered his method of review. A 1935 article in *Fortune* magazine noted:

On the priceless carpet at his feet there are spread six newspapers worth altogether from twelve to eighteen cents. . . . The old man—he is seventy-two—is hanging over them with a big black pencil in his hand. Every so often he reaches down and makes a cryptic black mark, with professional ease that smacks of the proofroom. The pencil moves and the marks look as if he were the head copyreader polishing off a final edition amid the rumble of presses under a green lamp shade in the small hours of the morning. Though you cannot hear the presses, he can. . . .

He rises now and then, paces along the edge of the newspapers, swooping down when he sees something to correct. . . .The job is finished. One week's work by an editor a few thousand miles away has been digested, corrected, and stored in that relentless memory.[7]

Mary Pickford, Charlie Chaplin, Gloria Swanson, Buddy Rogers, and D.W. Griffith were among this roomful of guests at Marion Davies's Santa Monica beach house.

Despite his heavy workload and the attention he devoted to San Simeon, Hearst still managed to produce a number of films. Although Cosmopolitan films were usually noted for their authentic period furnishings, two Hearst productions designed by Joseph Urban are recognized as the first use of the Art Deco style in films. *Enchantment* (1921) and *The Young Diana* (1922), both Davies pictures, were strikingly spare and reflective of the European trend toward the "moderne."[8]

Davies's 15th film, the 1922 production of *When Knighthood was in Flower,* was a critical and financial success. Reviewers for Hearst and non-Hearst papers were enthusiastic about her growth as an actress, the realistic sets

(dressed with authentic objects of the period furnished from Hearst's vast and various collections), and the supporting actors, including William Powell playing a black-hearted villain in his first screen performance.

Davies's success in this elaborate costume drama only reinforced Hearst's conviction that historical epics were the appropriate vehicle for Davies's climb to fame. This unfortunate predilection of Hearst's often masked Davies's comedic talents, leaving her stranded in a number of "costume clinkers," as critic Pauline Kael terms them. Hearst's continual emphasis on historical accuracy for props, sets, and costumes drove the budgets of her pictures skyward, making it virtually impossible for the films to turn a profit.

Never shy about publicizing his ventures, Hearst geared up his newspaper chain to ballyhoo Cosmopolitan's productions, and Davies's films in particular. Fulsome reviews, full-page rotogravures and extensive coverage of premieres were spread before audiences who were increasingly eager to know about the on- and off-screen activities of their favorite stars. Hearst's foray into serial films had taught him the value of multiple kinds of publicity. Hearst then conceived the notion of issuing new editions of the novels that Davies had filmed. A full-color dust jacket featured Davies in her movie role, while the title page announced the publication to be a "Marion Davies Edition."

The site of many celebrity parties, this beach house in Santa Monica was Marion Davies's home for many years. It was turned into a hotel after Hearst sold it in 1948. It has since been torn down.

The overblown publicity became the subject of mirth inside the film industry, capped by actress Beatrice Lillie's remark when first shown the lights of Los Angeles: "How wonderful!," said Lillie. "I suppose later they all merge and spell 'Marion Davies!'"[9]

One film historian, speculating on the reasons behind Davies's erratic box office drawing power, writes:

There are any number of explanations for Marion's troubles at the box office. She was a victim of her relationship with Hearst—a small portion of the public was offended by the unorthodox nature of the liaison—and she was also a victim of publicity overkill. Rarely a day went by without the Hearst papers mentioning her, usually with superlatives, and Davies served up daily with breakfast toast and coffee was too rich a diet for the average citizen.[10]

In 1924 Hearst joined the general exodus to California, moving Cosmopolitan Productions from its studio in New York's Harlem to Hollywood, where he made new alliances. At the conclusion of Paramount's contract to distribute Hearst's films, movie pioneer Samuel Goldwyn won the rights to release Cosmopolitan films, beginning with the 1923 Davies costume epic, *Little Old New York*. The other stars under contract to Cosmopolitan, including Alma Rubens and Lionel Barrymore, also came west.

This contract was perhaps Hearst's most strategic move in his movie-making ventures, as The Goldwyn Company merged within the year to form the infant Metro-Goldwyn-Mayer studio. Metro-Goldwyn-Mayer soon achieved preeminence as the most desirable and powerful of all Hollywood studios. Hearst's arrangement with MGM set a precedent in the industry. Cosmopolitan's feature films were distributed by MGM's parent company, Loew's, Inc., to their chain of theaters. According to the agreement, MGM bore the cost of producing all Cosmopolitan films and paid Davies a salary of $10,000 per week, an astronomical sum, matched only by the salaries of such popular stars as Chaplin and Pickford.

One of Hearst's ideas for promoting Marion Davies was to produce new editions of the novels she had filmed.

In return, Hearst agreed to split the profits of the Davies productions equally with MGM and to produce the *Hearst Metrotone News,* whose profits would also be divided in half. In addition, as perhaps the most important facet of the contract, Hearst agreed to publicize their productions and to provide designated MGM films with extensive publicity in his national newspaper chain. Hearst had the final decision on exactly which feature films received the coveted Cosmopolitan Productions imprimatur.[11]

In the years immediately following the Cosmopolitan/MGM partnership, Marion Davies gave her finest performances. Still turning out the costume dramas Hearst favored, Davies also found time to star in several comedies. The most successful of these, and widely regarded as her finest films, are two 1928 motion pictures, *The Patsy* and *Show People.* Both were directed by King Vidor, who had achieved great success with his epic films, *The Crowd* and *The Big Parade.* Once Vidor's reputation was established, Hearst did not rest until he had secured his services.[12]

Freed from the burdens of epic historical events and ponderous dialogue, Davies's skill as a light comedienne and gift for mimicry are fully evident in the Vidor comedies. *The Patsy,* a variation on the Cinderella theme, finds Davies slighted by her mother (Marie Dressler), who consistently favors Davies's glamorous sister. In the course of the plot, Davies renders deft and devastating impressions of three silent box office queens: Lillian Gish, Pola Negri, and Mae Murray.

Hearst's political ideas were directly expressed in his 1933 production entitled *Gabriel Over the White House.* The movie relates the story of President Jud Hammond (played by Walter Huston), whose ineffectual responses to the economic blight of the Depression satisfy only the corrupt political machine that secured his election. Through the intervention of a reporter (assisted by the angel Gabriel), Hammond abandons his passive Herbert Hooverish policies

and transforms himself into "a dictatorial presence made in differing parts of Theodore Roosevelt, Abraham Lincoln, and Huey Long. [Hammond] is granite in feature, solemn in word, aggressive in manner, and unconstitutional in action."[13]

He dismisses both Congress and his Cabinet and declares martial law in the name of expediency. The President creates a government-funded "Army of Construction" to employ the jobless, which in turn primes the nation's economy. Hammond eliminates gangsterism, the well-publicized "public enemy" of the period by repealing Prohibition and ordering the execution of the major mobster who resists his crackdown. Then, with movielike simplicity, "[Hammond's] earthly work is complete and there is no longer any need for a dictator. To reassure the audience that things will revert to the pre-Depression age, the film has Jud expire quite conveniently. He signs an international peace pact. . .with Lincoln's quill,. . .lapses into a coma [and] dies a martyr for his country."[14]

Both the screenwriter, Carey Wilson, and the producer, Walter Wanger, recall Hearst participating actively in this film, even to the point of writing or rewriting the Presidential speeches used in the movie. Hearst hoped the film would inspire additional public support for newly-elected President Franklin Delano Roosevelt.[15]

Hearst had not endorsed Roosevelt's Presidential aspirations until it became clear that his first choice, John Nance Garner of Texas, could not swing the necessary votes on the convention floor. Hearst agreed to release California's crucial delegates to Roosevelt in return for Garner's nomination as Vice-President. The crucial call was placed from the Gothic Library, Hearst's private San Simeon office, and Roosevelt was duly nominated.

Although he would soon break with Roosevelt, primarily over the issue of taxes on wealth, Hearst agreed with FDR that the first 100 days of the Roosevelt administration were crucial.[16] *Gabriel Over the White House,* containing several references to

Left: William Powell appeared with such stars as Rosalind Russell and Myrna Loy in the 1934 film, Evelyn Prentice, *an MGM/ Cosmopolitan production.*

Above: Henry Fonda and Marjorie Weaver in a scene from Young Mr. Lincoln, *a film produced in 1939 by 20th Century Fox in conjunction with Hearst.*

the recent 1932 Presidential campaign, was a direct effort on Hearst's part to smooth the path for the real-life President he had helped into office.

Cosmopolitan and MGM parted company in 1935 because Hearst believed that the choice roles (particularly Marie Antoinette and Elizabeth Barrett Browning) were going to Norma Shearer rather than to Marion Davies. Shearer was married to Irving Thalberg, the most powerful producer on the lot. Hearst thought leaving MGM and moving to Warner Brothers studio would remedy this situation. Louis B. Mayer, who valued Hearst's friendship as much as his influence, attempted to dissuade him, but failed. The well-publicized Davies dressing room (actually a 14-room house) was cut into sections and hauled on several flatbed trucks across the Hollywood hills to her new studio.

By the spring of 1937 Hearst was upset about the lack of starring roles suitable for Davies. Ella ("Bill") Williams, the Cosmopolitan liaison at the studio, wrote to Jack Warner about the situation, warning, "[Hearst] said one thing that Metro did was to get stories for Marion, realizing that she was a star and the stories were about and for her. . . .He said that he has been very unhappy on this last picture [*Ever Since Eve* with Robert Montgomery], fighting for everything he has gotten and. . .[still] having Marion look like a stick. . . .He said, 'Maybe this is what [the Warner brothers] want here. Maybe they would prefer getting out of our contract.'"[17] Davies decided to retire, but Hearst moved his production company to Twentieth Century-Fox, where he produced *Young Mr. Lincoln*. The association with Twentieth Century-Fox lasted two years.

Clockwise from top left:

1. Marion Davies, Clark Gable, and Eileen Percy dressed as children at a birthday party held at Marion's Santa Monica beach house.

2. A group that called itself "The Flying San Simeons" and included film stars Cary Grant (third from right) and Randolph Scott (second from right), performed acrobatic stunts at a circus party.

3. Hearst with party guests Douglas Fairbanks, Mary Pickford, Charlie Chaplin, and Pola Negri.

4. Hearst with Hedda Hopper (left) and Adela Rogers St. Johns (right).

5. Marie Dressler and Harpo Marx at a bon voyage party given by Davies in honor of Norma Shearer.

Hearst broadcasting in the 1930s.

Hearst's influence as a film producer, coupled with his media power, made him an important member of Hollywood society. San Simeon, although located over 250 miles north of the studios, was a social mecca to denizens of the film colony. Those who received the coveted invitations were drawn from a wide circle of friends, family, Hearst executives, politicians, journalists, celebrities, athletes, as well as directors, producers, and stars in the motion picture industry. Actors playing opposite Marion Davies were often invited to the hilltop estate to rehearse for an extended period of time. The only recourse for those not invited to the estate was to read about it in the popular press. *Fortune* magazine offered this description of a San Simeon visit for its readers in 1931:

The Southern Pacific Railway, running between Los Angeles and San Francisco. . .circles inward at San Luis Obispo. Here. . .the private train which brings the Hearst guests rests on a siding. . . .Pilgrims of the private train, arising leisurely, are motored. . .forty-three miles and, at San Simeon, turn inland and ascend to the castle [high] above in the hills. . . . The road up [is] a beautiful, wide, carefully-laid gravel road whose windings flatten a slope so steep that [as a child] Hearst clung to the tail of a horse to be pulled up. . . .

At the base of this hill you passed the airfield on which may land late Hearst newspapers from [distant] cities. . . . Continue on up the road, through what will be Sequoia forests a thousand-odd years from now, then give it one last swing and end it. . . .Standing there, you can look back, out over the hills to the Pacific; then look around you to find Moorish palaces amid enchanted gardens. . .set off by the great twin towers of the Spanish mission cathedral which is La Casa Grande. You are now in the heart of the Hearst estate.[18]

The Castle's Refectory, which was decorated with a portion of Hearst's vast silver collection.

Adela Rogers St. Johns, a respected writer for newspapers, magazines, and films, made her first trip to San Simeon with Hearst himself, even though she was nervous about traveling with a boss she believed to be distant. St. Johns overcame her awe and was soon engaged in lively conversation with her boss:

We went into a roadside diner at Los Alamos and sat on stools and Mr. Hearst said he recommended the ham and eggs or the chili so I had both. Then we got back on the road. Coming out of San Luis Obispo. . .we ran into. . .fog,. . .which thickened so the car had to cut through it like a knife. . . .Mr. Hearst said, "Here's a shoulder, pull off and I will drive."

. . .Here we have a trained chauffeur, it's his business, *I said to myself. Mr. William Randolph Hearst owns gold mines and runs 999 newspapers and can tell presidents what to do so he thinks he can drive. . . .*

Fifty miles to San Simeon. Though from time to time I heard a car or the rocks bouncing down from the cliff edge, I never saw anything. Our way was as wide as the car's wheels, no wider, and as spiral as a corkscrew. We drove at a steady, fast pace, once or twice we stopped to let a gate swing open under the invisible guidance of a Mexican cowboy, we curved, climbed without a single hesitation or inch of deviation, and came to a perfect stop on the circular drive in front of what we then called the Three Cottages.

On the terrace of one of the white-stucco three-story "cottages" that were the only houses then finished, Mr. Hearst bowed and told me a courteous good night and thanked me for my company.[19]

It is still widely believed that Hearst was so phobic about death that it could not be mentioned in his presence. St. Johns believes the origin of this myth derived from the popular song, "(I'll Be Glad When You're Dead) You Rascal, You." One evening after the movie screening, some of the younger guests played the record "over and *over.* At a point of nausea, Mr. Hearst removed it, broke it in two, and put the pieces in the fireplace saying, 'I feel we have heard that often enough. I find it a vulgar lyric

An article in the October 11, 1940, San Francisco Examiner *describes the unveiling of the "Bear Fountain" at Wyntoon, Hearst's estate in northern California.*

and a vapid tune. Let us have something gay.'"[20]

Harry Crocker, a friend of Hearst's who stayed at San Simeon for extended periods, recalls a dinner conversation about the possibility of life after death. Hearst calmly ventured two opinions. "Either there is something, in which case we can only speculate and wait," said Hearst, "or there's nothing, in which case there's nothing to worry about."[21]

Actor Joel McCrea, a frequent guest of Hearst's in the 1930s, recalls that the always impressive guest list kept dinnertime conversation flowing. At one noteworthy birthday party Hearst was toasted with champagne by the head of every major movie studio in Hollywood. At another dinner party, McCrea found himself seated between Amelia Earhart and Charles Lindbergh. At yet another gathering, McCrea conversed with an older woman who was dressed very simply. He then discovered her name was Julia Morgan and that his mother had attended the University of California at Berkeley with her.

Still exchanging stories, Morgan and McCrea left the Refectory. "I put my arm around her and was talking about my mother. . . .Mr. Hearst saw that, so he came up to me afterward. Usually he was aloof of most things, unless it was [Arthur] Brisbane or something, but. . .he came up and said, 'How did you happen to know Miss Morgan? She's my architect. . .she takes castles down in Spain and puts them on a boat and sends them back.' And I said, 'Well, she [and] my mother graduated [together] and they were Kappa Alpha Beta and roommates. . . .'" From that moment, Hearst took special interest in the actor's career, even interceding (without McCrea's knowledge) on his behalf to studio chief Louis B. Mayer.[22]

Given Hearst's interest in the motion picture industry and the preponderance of guests who worked within it, the tradition of screening a new film each evening began at San Simeon. Adela Rogers St. Johns remembers, "There was a motion picture run every single night come hell or high water. . .and to this every guest whether exalted or unimportant had to go. And *stay*. . . .This was, I think, partly because Mr. Hearst loved movies and partly because he had a sort of paternal care for his high-spirited and temperamental guests and thought it might be dangerous for them to wander about at night, alone or in couples. (It often was.)"[23]

By early 1937 Hearst's financial condition, both personal and business, was precarious. The advent of Roosevelt's New Deal and a sharp rise in taxes on personal wealth and large corporations, coupled with Hearst's unrestrained buying sprees, had all contributed to his financial woes. It was estimated that there were at least 90 companies under the Hearst Corporation name and each had borrowed from banks and other Hearst companies until the indebtedness was estimated at $126 million.[24]

John Francis Neylan, a Hearst friend and advisor once was quoted as saying, "Money as such bores him. . . .He is a builder. He wants to build buildings, newspapers, magazines, hotels, ranches. His idea is to build, build, build all the time. . . .In his makeup there is just a blank space in relation to money."[25] Hearst's "blank space" was soon filled with the advice of lawyers and financial consultants. In June of 1937, Hearst signed over his controlling stock in the primary holding corporation to Judge Clarence J. Shearn, a friend and lawyer for the past 37 years. Hearst retained control of editorial policy, but his finances were now in other hands for the first time since Phoebe Hearst had bestowed the proceeds from the Anaconda mines on him almost 45 years earlier.

Hearst on steps of St. Donat's, his castle in Wales, which he purchased in 1925.

Shearn directed the sale of the six Hearst papers that operated at a deficit along with seven of the 10 Hearst radio stations. Only one Hearst magazine, *Pictorial Review*, ceased publication; Hearst's two wire services were merged into one company. In the first year Shearn managed to save the Corporation $5 million.

It was less easy to persuade Hearst to part with his vast treasure trove of antiquities or his magnificent estates. The advisors recommended that at least two-thirds of the art must be sold to avoid inheritance taxes and to provide a cash infusion to the corporation. Appraisers determined that Hearst had collected 504 separate categories of art, 20 of which were outstanding. Hearst's accumulation of English silver, armor, English furniture, tapestries, and Hispano-Moresque pottery were ranked among the finest private collections in the world.

The 5th floor of Gimbel Brothers department store was transformed, according to the *Saturday Evening Post*, into a "gigantic bazaar of the arts." Ten thousand art objects, including paneling, ceilings, stained glass, paintings, and sculpture, covered

These candid photographs of Hearst and his guests at St. Donat's ran in The Graphic, *a British magazine.*

100,000 square feet of space in the store. The initial two-month period, during which Gimbels' assumed the role of agent and received a commission on each piece sold, was so successful it was extended for 14 months. The *New York Times* noted, "Armor, of which Hearst had enough to stage a successful siege of his castle of St. Donat, sold from $4.50 up. Egyptian statuettes, tagged at 35, 60 and 95 cents, were among the fifteen thousand items. . . ." The English silver, including pieces from the Tudor, Stuart, and early Georgian periods, were sold at Sotheby's London office.

Also sold during the period of retrenchment was a 12th century Cistercian monastery Hearst had purchased outright in 1925. Hearst had commissioned an art dealer, Arthur Byne, to locate and purchase a Gothic cloister. Byne investigated Sacramenia, where he discovered the entire monastery was available. All of the structures were dismantled stone by stone (with the exception of the kitchen and the lay brothers' refectory) and shipped to New York in numbered crates.

The straw that was used as packing material was banned by the U.S. Agricultural Department, forcing the stones to be uncrated and repacked before they left Spain. The cost of the shipping alone was estimated at $400,000. Hearst's plans to reconstruct the monastery were abandoned after his financial difficulties in the late 1930s. Eventually the stones were sold for $19,000 and shipped to North Miami Beach, Florida, where the building was reconstructed as an Episcopalian church.[26]

Another Hearst estate, on the McCloud River in northern California, was named Wyntoon. A favorite retreat of Phoebe Hearst's, the Wyntoon property was originally a part of the Charles W. Wheeler estate. Although Wheeler did not wish to sell any of the land, Phoebe Hearst ardently wished for an "inexpensive little house" there. Wheeler agreed to let her build, provided the house cost a maximum of $10,000. Revision and enlargement of the plans drawn by noted California architect Bernard Maybeck led to a house that cost 10 times the original figure.[27]

When fire claimed a portion of the estate in 1929, Hearst retained Morgan to design yet another village-sized retreat on the 50,000 acre site. Here Hearst envisioned the perfect setting for some of his first collections, including the German beer steins and Swiss wood carvings he acquired on his first trip to Europe nearly 60 years earlier. Morgan's Wyntoon was decidedly Bavarian. Artist Willy Pogany drew large murals depicting German fairy tales.

Half a mile down the river from Hearst's Bear House was The Gables, where ". . .Hearst guests live, eat, drink, and make merry. It. . .perches on the edge of the river, a friendly, rambling, Alpine-like structure of stucco and bare beams. Within its pine-paneled walls are the dining room for sixty guests; a lounge with a great fireplace and a smattering of modern furniture. Also that indispensable item of Hearst home equipment—the cinema theatre."[28]

Top: Detail of mural on the front of Bear House.

Bottom: The original Hearst residence at Wyntoon, designed by Bernard Maybeck.

Opposite top: Bear House is nestled between the towering cedar, fir, and pine trees.

Opposite bottom: River House is perched on the edge of the roaring McCloud River.

In 1930, Arthur Byne located another monastery for Hearst, the Santa Maria de Ovila, which was erected near Burgos, Spain, sometime before 1213. Byne once again began the laborious process of dismantling and shipping the stones to San Francisco while Julia Morgan began to draw plans that would incorporate the monastery into the expansion of Wyntoon. A barn-sized structure used to store wine was contemplated as a future movie theater. The long and exceedingly narrow main building was once considered for a living room, but existing Morgan plans illustrate its proposed conversion into an indoor swimming pool.

By the time the monastery arrived on 11 ships in San Francisco harbor, Hearst's financial difficulties precluded any of these plans. A fire in the warehouse where the stones were stored obliterated the numbering system, making it impossible to reconstruct the monastery. All that remains of Santa Maria de Ovila is the rubble in San Francisco's Golden Gate Park.

Left: The Milpitas Hacienda was another of architect Julia Morgan's designs.
Above: Hearst's Milpitas Hacienda near Jolon served as a rest stop during his lengthy horseback trips.

Hearst's widow and their five sons shortly after his death.

Hearst's financial pressures also curtailed building at San Simeon. He had followed George Hearst's practice of buying parcels of land from neighbors, until his holdings at San Simeon approached 260,000 acres. Columnist Hedda Hopper remembered:

> One day when I was standing on the balcony outside the library showing Lady Irene Ravensdale how much land W.R. owned, I swept my arm in a circle and said, "He owns all of these 375,000 [sic] acres except that mountain away off there in the distance." Then a thin voice came over my shoulder, "Hedda, I own that, too."[30]

In addition to the construction on the seaside hilltop at San Simeon, in the late 1920s Hearst decided to build a (relatively) small hacienda at the northern boundaries of his ranch. Located some 25 miles north of La Cuesta Encantada near the tiny settlement of Jolon, the hacienda was built primarily to serve as an oasis for Hearst and the visitors who chose to accompany him on strenuous horseback tours of his sprawling ranch.

Less than a mile from the newest Hearst hacienda lay the Mission San Antonio de Padua. Contained on Hearst property, the Mission had been in a state of disrepair following the secularization of the missions, and completely abandoned after 1882. Phoebe Hearst and her son both contributed to the restoration of the historic structure when the drive to preserve California's 21 missions became a popular effort at the turn of the century. Julia Morgan directed the restoration efforts at Mission San Antonio. A great deal of this acreage, including the Milpitas hacienda, was sold to the U.S. Army in the early 1940s.

During World War II, Hearst spent a great deal of his time at Wyntoon because it was generally believed that San Simeon was vulnerable to Japanese attack. After the war he returned to San Simeon, but in 1947 a heart attack forced him to leave the estate for the last time. He retreated to a relatively modest Beverly Hills estate at 1007 Lexington Drive to be close to the specialists who attempted to maintain his faltering health.

By the mid-1930s Hearst's real estate holdings were almost as vast as his journalistic empire. Hearst owned 27 acres of Manhattan real estate that he planned to develop as the headquarters for the Hearst Corporation. Working with his star editor and friend, Arthur Brisbane, Hearst envisioned the development as a rival to the newly-built Rockefeller Center. But Hearst and Brisbane were caught in the financial cataclysms of the early Depression years and their plans came to nothing. Other Manhattan property owned by Hearst included the Ritz Tower, where he retained a private floor for his New York visits; two other hotels, the Warwick and the Lombardy; Sherwood Studios; and the Ziegfeld and Cosmopolitan theaters. The Hearst Corporation also owned newspaper buildings in 18 other cities.[29]

The inside of San Francisco's Grace Cathedral, where 1,500 people attended Hearst's funeral in August 1951.

On August 14, 1951, William Randolph Hearst died at the age of 88 from "several cerebral vascular accidents" together with the effects of "ailments of advanced age." His widow and five sons gathered for the funeral in San Francisco and the interment at Cypress Lawn Cemetery in Colma, California. His will, at 125 pages, was the longest ever filed in California. A portion of the estate, believed to total nearly $220 million, was left in trust to his family; the remainder was bequeathed as a charitable trust.

Headlines in newspapers around the world marked his passing. National magazines struggled with the task of interpreting his personality and analyzing the impact of his various careers. *Life* magazine, in a 10-page obituary, theorized, ". . .Hearst was more than a man; he was the inventor, purveyor, prolificator and practitioner of a phenomenon known as Hearst Journalism. . . .In part it was a one-man fireworks display. . . ."[31]

But for all his wealth, influence, and exposure, Hearst remains an enigmatic figure, a man whose public character and private inclinations have been little known and even less understood. His energies and enthusiasms outstripped every competitor; his name still inspires debate. Perhaps the only person who was not mystified was Hearst himself. "If I had my life to live over again," remarked William Randolph Hearst, "I would be a newspaper man, and merely try to be a better one."[32]

Part Four Endnotes

1 Joseph Willicombe to J.B. Lee, March 23, 1921 and draft response from Julia Morgan (JM) to WRH, [1921]; both from JM Collection, Cal Poly.

2 WRH to JM, February 7, 1927, JM Collection, Cal Poly.

3 WRH to JM, February 19, 1927, JM Collection, Cal Poly.

4 WRH to JM, June 2, 1921, JM Collection, Cal Poly.

5 JM to WRH, May 19, 1924, JM Collection, Cal Poly.

6 Harry Bitner, "Hearst Was Last of Great Individualists," *Editor & Publisher* August 18, 1951, 13.

7 "Hearst," *Fortune* October, 1935, 43.

8 Howard Mandelbaum and Eric Myers, *Screen Deco* (New York: St. Martin's Press, 1985) 7.

9 Charlie Chaplin, *My Autobiography* (New York: Simon & Shuster, 1964) 331.

10 Gary Carey, *All the Stars in Heaven* (New York: E.P. Dutton, 1981) 114-15.

11 Bernard Rosenberg and Harry Silverstein, *The Real Tinsel* (London: The Macmillan Company, 1970) 114.

12 Tom Milne, "Show People" *Sight and Sound* 37 (Fall, 1968) 200-201.

13 Andrew Bergman, *We're in the Money: Depression America and Its Films* (New York: Harper & Row, 1972) 111. The powerful contemporary columnist Walter Lippmann disliked the film, stating "as a sample of what the movies can do for the political education of mankind, *Gabriel* is not so promising. . . .*Gabriel* is the infantile world of irresistible wishes. More specifically, it is a dramatization of Mr. Hearst's editorials." *Motion Picture Herald*, April 8, 1933, 1.

14 Peter Roffman and Jim Purdy, *The Hollywood Social Problem Film: Madness, Despair, and Politics from the Depression to the Fifties* (Bloomington: Indiana University Press, 1981) 69.

15 Samuel Marx, *Mayer and Thalberg: The Make-Believe Saints* (New York: Random House, 1975) 204. See also Roffman and Purdy 71-72.

16 Rodney Carlisle, "William Randolph Hearst: A Fascist Reputation Reconsidered" *Journalism Quarterly* 50.1 (1973) 127-133.

17 Memo from Ella Williams to J.L. Warner quoted in Rudy Behlmer, ed., *Inside Warner Bros. 1935-1951* (New York: Viking Press, 1985) 38.

18 "Hearst at Home," *Fortune* May, 1931, 57.

19 St. Johns 124-128.

20 St. Johns 140.

21 "Small Talk About Big People," ts. of pp. 61-63, Harry Crocker Collection, Margaret Herrick Library, Academy of Motion Picture Arts and Sciences.

22 Interview with Joel McCrea conducted by Metta Hake, December 5, 1982, pp. 6-13. Courtesy of Hearst San Simeon State Historical Monument.

23 St. Johns 140.

24 Winkler 278.

25 Winkler 1.

26 Joanne E. Sowell, "The Monastery of Sacramenia and Twelfth-Century Cisterian Architecture in Spain". Diss. Florida State University, 1985, 59-69. Sowell comments at length on the secrecy that surrounded the removal of an historical monument from Spain. Byne instructed both Morgan and Hearst never to mention the name of the monastery in their cables.

27 Undated memorandum, PAH Papers, Bancroft.

28 "Hearst," *Fortune* October, 1935, 44.

29 "Hearst Once Owned 2,000,000 Acres," *Editor & Publisher* August 18, 1951, 10.

30 "Hedda Hopper's Hollywood" ts. of press release for August 29, 1957, Hedda Hopper Collection, Margaret Herrick Library, Academy of Motion Picture Arts and Sciences. The State Department of Parks and Recreation (formerly the State Division of Parks and Beaches) has managed the Monument since the transfer of ownership. On June 2, 1958, the Monument opened to the public for the first time.

31 *Life* August 27, 1951, 22.

32 Winkler 1.

Visiting Hearst San Simeon State Historical Monument

Visitors to the Monument are encouraged to tour the Visitor Center, which was completed in 1987. The Center houses exhibits that graphically portray some of the many facets of the life and times of William Randolph Hearst. Additional displays introduce you to the beautiful scenery and other attractions of California's Central Coast. A ticket office, souvenir shop, and snack bar are also located in the complex. Of special interest is an observation area for watching art conservators and staff as they restore some of the many art objects housed at the castle.

A five-mile bus ride transports you from the Visitor Center, across the Hearst ranch lands, and up to the Castle. During the ride, it is not uncommon to see such remaining vestiges of Hearst's menagerie as zebras, tahr and aoudad goats, and fallow deer. At the top of the hill, an expert tour guide leads you and your group through the Castle's buildings and grounds, beginning with the outdoor Neptune Pool and ending at the indoor Roman Pool. Each of the four tour routes follows a different path. We recommend Tour One to first-time visitors because it is an excellent introduction to the Castle. Reservations are suggested as tours often sell out in advance. For additional information write to:

Hearst San Simeon State Historical Monument
P.O. Box 8
San Simeon, CA 93452-0040.

GENERAL TOUR INFORMATION

- The Monument is open for tours daily except for Thanksgiving, Christmas, and New Year's Days.

- Tour One is recommended for first-time visitors.

- Tickets are sold for specific tour times. Your tour leaves the Visitor Center at the time printed on your ticket.

- Walking distance for each tour is approximately one-half mile. In addition, each tour requires that you climb and/or descend 150 to 350 steps.

- Each tour lasts one hour and forty-five minutes.

- Due to the narrow hallways and numerous steps, large or bulky backpacks, camera bags, purses, and strollers are not allowed on the tours.

- Visitors may take photographs on the grounds and in the buildings. Tripods as well as any type of flash equipment are not permitted. Commercial photographers must make special arrangements directly with the Monument prior to their arrival.